1001 little
fashion miracles

1001 little fashion miracles

Esme Floyd

CARLTON
BOOKS

THIS IS A CARLTON BOOK

Text and design copyright ©
Carlton Books Limited 2008
Illustrations copyright © Carol Morley

This edition published by
Carlton Books Limited
20 Mortimer Street
London W1T 3JW

A CIP catalogue record for this book is available
from the British Library.

ISBN: 978 1 84442 838 0

Printed and bound in Dubai

Senior Executive Editor: Lisa Dyer
Managing Art Director: Lucy Coley
Design: Anna Pow
Illustrator: Carol Morley
Production: Kate Pimm

CONTENTS

INTRODUCTION

Did you know that slingback shoes flatter everyone or that the right underwear can take off 10 lbs (4.5 kg) , or even that a wide belt can help give you a waist if you have a boyish figure?

From tips for creating a capsule wardrobe and dressing for your particular body shape to finding the right shoe for your outfit or the best date dress, this book contains 1001 little marvels to show you how small changes in what you wear can make a huge difference to your appearance. Advice on solving fashion disasters and fashion secrets from top stylists are also included to help you look polished, groomed and gorgeous from head to toe – whether you go.

Top ten little fashion miracles

5
FOOTWEAR FOR WORK
(see Shoes, page 9)

37
KEEP IT CLASSIC
(see Handbags, page 16)

105
BELT IT
(see Scarves, wraps & belts, page 30)

222
CALL IN THE PROFESSIONALS
(see Lovely lingerie, page 59)

276
GROUP IT
(see Organizing your wardrobe, page 72)

289
BALANCING ACT
(see Looking slimmer, page 78)

341
MAKE A CROSSOVER
(see Dressing for hourglass figures, page 90)

500
GET THE DETAILS RIGHT
(see Date clothes, page 123)

698
THREE CRUCIAL QUESTIONS
(see Sensible shopping, page 166)

881
FLATTEN YOUR TUM
(see Stylists' secrets, page 201)

shoes

1 SAY IT WITH SHOES

Shoes have symbolic meaning so make a statement with them – they're more important than jewellery, sunglasses or any other accessory.

2 BEWARE ANKLE BOOTS

Boots that stop just above the ankle can be difficult to wear with dresses or skirts as they cut off the leg at the slenderest point. Unless you are very thin and the shoe is very form-fitting, your best bet is to go for the lower-cut shoe boot.

3 NO-NOS FOR MINIS

Never team heavy shoes with minis; especially avoid Oxford shoes, clogs or bulky shoes, which will make your feet look huge in comparison. Although padded cross-trainers (sneakers) are a definite no-no, trainers can be cute when worn with minis or denim skirts. Choose plimsolls like Keds for a preppy look or Converses for a sceney urban style.

4 BELT UP

Although shoes and handbags don't have to match to look good these days, belts and shoes do tend to look better if they coordinate. A black belt with a brown pair of shoes (and vice versa) simply looks as though you're not trying. They don't have to be exactly the same colour and fabric but aim for the same colour family.

5 FOOTWEAR FOR WORK

Slingback shoes are the most universally flattering style and a good option to wear with trousers, skirts, dresses or suits for work. Because they are sophisticated, yet a touch sexy, they are the perfect choice for the career woman who wants to still feel and look feminine.

6 BEST FOOT FORWARD

The old adage that people can tell a lot about you by the shoes you wear is true. Scuffs or battered or damaged shoes and worn heels all say you don't care as much as you should about life's important details.

7 TREAT YOUR FEET

You don't have to suffer to look great in heels – buy shoes that are slightly roomier so you can add gel inserts for extra comfort under the balls of your feet. Most pharmacies sell them and they fit neatly into your handbag for sore-feet emergencies.

8 COLOUR CODING

Although we all need a few pairs of neutral shoes in our wardrobe, forget the rule that says shoes always have to match your handbag. Matching colours can be a bit tacky but do make sure your shoes go with your outfit and are not too dark or too light in tone. A good rule is to match them to one of the less dominant colours in your outfit, be that a swirl of colour in your skirt print or even a bead in your earrings.

9 BE BOLD

Take risks: if you like looking edgy you can clash your shoes with your outfit – for example, wearing red shoes with a pink dress. But be warned: it takes a sure hand and plenty of confidence to carry this off.

10 BIKER BOOT STYLE

Biker boots never really go out of style as they are practical, comfortable, hard-wearing and versatile. The favourite types, such as Belstaff, are highly sought-after but there are many other brands. With their distinctive cut and style, motorcycle boots add an edgy hardcore look to casual outfits.

11 PLATFORM POWER

High-rise platforms are a strong look and can add height without discomfort. Slim-heeled versions look good with suits or evening dresses while chunkier styles are fun and adventurous. The most comfortable types are those where the sole actually bends when you walk – where the platform is restricted to the areas at the ball of the foot and the heel.

12 MINIMIZE YOUR SIZE

Bright is bigger so be aware that your feet can look larger in block-coloured shoes. If you hate the size of your feet, opt for neutrals instead. If you have wide feet, choose pointy-toed shoes, which help the foot look narrower.

13 RIDE 'EM HIGH COWBOY

The cowboy trend goes in and out of fashion but always seems to come back at some point in a slightly different styling. Whether you wear them with skirts or jeans, keep the other Western styling details to a minimum – no turquoise jewellery, cowboy hats or large belt buckles.

16 THE VERSATILE WEDGE

More comfortable than stilettos, wedge sandals are a fantastic summer choice for wearing with dresses, jeans, gauchos or even shorts if you've got the legs. Wedges can also be found on boot and pump styles in materials ranging from casual suedes and textured materials to fine leathers and metallics.

14 BOOT IT IN

Forget spiky heels in winter and inclement weather and instead choose shoe boots. Low-cut shoe boots are a less bulky choice than other boots for wearing under trousers or skinny jeans and look modern when worn with short skirts or dresses.

17 MATCH LIGHTNESS

Strappy sandals are the favourite choice for formal eveningwear where even open-toed or peep shoes will look too heavy. If the look is light – your dress is floaty or exposing – your shoes should reflect it. Bronze, silver or gold sandals are good choices, but make sure you match the metallic colour to your jewellery and any hardware on your bags.

15 MATCHPOINT

We all know shop assistants are constantly trying to palm us off with expensive shoe cleaner whenever we buy a new pair, but if you're buying an unusual shade, it's worth investing in the polish to match at the same time as you buy your shoes rather than having to hunt for it weeks later at the first sign of a scuff.

18 HEEL KNOW-HOW

The thicker the heel tip, the more comfortable and stable the shoes will feel. Small heels, especially stilettos, will wear down more quickly.

19 SUMMERTIME SHOES

Kitten heels and slingbacks are great choices for summer wear when you don't want to show your toes or the weather's a bit chilly or rainy. They look good with either trousers or skirts.

20 MAKE MINE A MARY JANE

Originally an Edwardian shoe with a round toe, strap and buckle, and a popular choice for the 'little girl' look, Mary Janes are now most often seen as stack-heel styles. The updated MJ, such as the two-tone type by Marc Jacobs, is much more versatile than the traditional styles as it has very high heels and looks good with skirts or trousers.

21 PUT COMFORT FIRST

High heels push your weight forward onto the balls of your feet so check to see how cushioned this area is before you hand over your credit card.

22 TRY THE TOE TEST

With closed toes, make sure you can still wiggle your toes. If you can't do this, the shoes are too tight and may cut off your circulation – leading to numb toes by the end of the night. Tight shoes can also lead to ingrown toenails and bunions.

23 HOT FEET

Always try on shoes towards the end of a shopping trip when your feet are at their hottest and most swollen to get a better idea of how they will fit.

24 PERFECTLY PAINTED

Never wear open-toed sandals with chipped nail polish or unkempt toenails. If you're going to expose your feet, give yourself a pedicure and paint your toenails the night before.

25 PICK THE PERFECT HEEL

Even if you're a little on the short side, don't be tempted to go for killer heels all the time – they can make you totter and look as though you're trying too hard. Instead, try wearing medium-sized or kitten heels, which provide the ideal combination of height to give you confidence and elegance to elongate your legs.

26 BE WELL-HEELED

Don't wait until the last minute to have your shoes heeled. You're more likely to do permanent damage by scuffing the leather base. If you have a favourite pair of shoes that you wear regularly, put a date in your diary every six to eight weeks to drop them into your nearest shoe repair shop.

27 BOOTS MADE FOR WALKING

A great pair of knee-high boots is the ultimate footwear and they can be worn with just about anything. Knee-high boots look great under or over jeans, and with short or long skirts and dresses, so invest in a well-fitting, good-quality leather pair that will last and last. For a casual look, slip on the celebrity favourite Ugg boots – they are super-snug and look great with jeans or denim skirts.

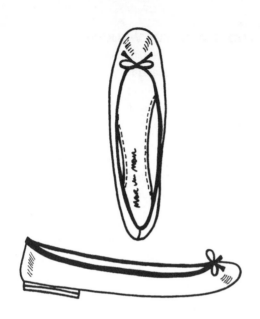

29 PUMP UP THE VOLUME

Flat shoes such as ballet pumps look lovely when worn with short skirts and minis, but never wear them with longer skirts. Flat shoes can appear to add weight to the leg but this is counterbalanced by exposing more area of the leg.

30 DOUBLE DUTY

Similarly check if any of your shoes need new soles or heels and drop them off at your local shoe bar. To save time, choose an outlet that does dry-cleaning as well – so you can have both chores done at once.

28 BE PREPARED

Put together a simple shoe repair kit that contains polish for every shade of shoes that you wear, a protector spray for suede and nubuck plus a suede brush, and trainer (sneaker) whitener. Once a month give all your shoes a good clean and polish to make sure they look presentable.

31 SHOE SHAPERS

Ideally, keep all your shoes in shoe trees when not in use. This will extend their life, maintain their shape, prevent creases and keep them dry. Renowned for its aroma and drying properties, cedarwood is the best material for shoe trees as it's ideal for keeping footwear fresh and dry. Cedar will absorb foot moisture, acids and salts and reduce cracking and deterioration.

32 DARE TO BARE

Most fashion experts agree that there's nothing worse than wearing sheer tan tights with sandals, so plan ahead and shave or wax your legs and apply fake tan the night before. Block-colour opaque tights, on the other hand, can look cool with chunky platform sandals.

33 BE SEXY WITH PEEP TOES

If you don't happen to like exposing your feet, or think they are unattractive, get a sexy look by wearing peep toes. These styles cover up quite a lot of the foot but have a suggestive cut-away area at the toe.

34 TIGHT FIT

Showing off bare white legs in winter looks nasty, not to mention unprofessional for work, so invest in lots of pairs of funky patterned tights. Not only do they add colour and fun to an outfit, but they also hide a multitude of sins!

handbags

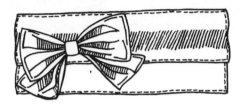

35 THE RIGHT BAG

You can really transform an outfit with a stylish bag. The choice is endless but suede is great for daytime while gold and silver leather add instant evening chic.

36 COPYCAT

Fake designer bags are hard to spot but there are a number of features to look out for. Check the colour of the stitching as this should match the bag perfectly with no fraying. Pay attention to the quality and weight of decorative parts such as chains, while the logo should be engraved and not embossed on the material; it should also feature on the inside lining.

37 KEEP IT CLASSIC

If you are lucky enough to afford a designer bag, it's much more of an investment to go for a style that will stand the test of time rather than the latest 'it' bag. Look for classic shapes and colours such as black or tan.

38 CLUTCH CONTROL

Swapping your normal day bag for a cute clutch is an easy way to dress up your work outfit for a night out. Choose snakeskin or sequined styles for a touch of glamour.

39 A WHITER SHADE OF PALE

White bags look wonderful but remember they will become grubby faster than any other colour. If you really can't resist, keep them for special occasions, not everyday use. Beige or baby blue is a good alternative that won't highlight dirt in quite the same way.

40 BAG A GREAT WAISTLINE

If you have a tiny waist, choose a bag that hangs just above it: this will draw the eye to that particular area and helps accentuate it.

41 TLC FOR BAGS

To keep expensive handbags looking their best, store them in drawstring cotton bags when not in use and keep them in the top of your wardrobe – rather than at the bottom with shoes – to prevent them from being squashed out of shape.

42 BE FORMAL WITH A FRAME

Bags that are highly structured with a metal frame support were very fashionable in the 1950s and can be used to create a very pulled-together, groomed look, especially if made in crocodile or calfskin. The famous Hermès Kelly bag is an example, though the shape doesn't always need to be square or trapezoidal.

43 FIRST IMPRESSIONS COUNT

For interviews and meetings, make sure your bag is functional and smart. Choose one that can easily hold a CV (résumé) or business proposal, as well as having pockets to keep business cards, pens and your phone easily accessible – so you're not scrabbling around for them.

44 BOOST YOUR CURVES

If you want to maximize your cleavage, choose a bag with short straps that hangs just under your armpit. This will draw attention to the area and give the impression of a bigger bust.

45 PICK A HOBO

A good everyday choice is the hobo handbag. Roomy and slouchy, it has a short shoulder strap to allow a snug fit under the arm, making it hard for purse-snatchers to grab and keeping contents safe and secure.

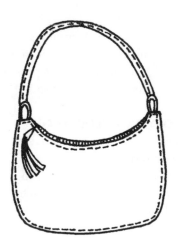

46 MATCH THE SEASONS

Think carefully about which fabrics are right for which season. Velvet and dark leather bags are great for winter, while in summer try bags made from wicker, cotton and brightly coloured leather.

47 COMPLEMENT FOR COMPLIMENTS

While it's now considered old-fashioned to perfectly match your bag to your shoes, on occasions when smart dress is required, check they complement each other with similar shades and textures.

48 WEAR AND CARE

Keep leather and suede bags in top condition by treating them with waterproof sprays once a month, and where possible avoid using them in rainy weather.

49 ACCESSORY, NOT NECESSITY

When buying a bag for a party or special occasion, look on it as an accessory to your outfit rather than a necessity to stuff essentials into. Beaded or sequined bags always add extra glamour.

50 PERSONALIZE YOUR BAG

If you like to keep things simple, look for a small bag that won't cramp your style. Practical and always on the move? You need something that reflects your busy lifestyle, so look for structured bags with several pockets to accommodate your ever-changing needs. And if you're an extrovert, a big, bold oversized bag is the ideal choice to suit your style and needs.

51 REMEMBER PROPORTION

When choosing a new bag, always try it on in front of a mirror as the style may not suit the proportions of your body. Oversized bags can look ridiculous on very tiny or short women and they can also hide or block you and your clothing from view. Likewise, tiny bags on big women can look silly. Think about the overall look the bag creates on your body.

52 MATCH YOUR LOOK

Make sure the style of your bag suits the outfit you are wearing. When you are going for a girly look, don't choose a black studded leather bag; similarly, a bright red patent bag is great for 'rock chick' style but floral cotton won't work at all.

53 BAGS OF FUN

When you want to make a statement, look for bags with unusual detailing such as feathers, studs, fake fur and embroidery. If the colours are neutral, they will go with any outfit but still catch the eye and make an impact.

54 IN THE NAVY

Navy bags are a good alternative to black in spring and summer. They sharpen up office clothes and work with red, tan and cream.

55 SIZE MATTERS

If you're not blessed with height, pick short bags that hang close to the body to create the illusion of being taller than you really are.

56 JUNK IT

Make sure you set aside time to regularly de-clutter your handbag. Fact: some of us carry up to 3.5 kg (7 lb) of personal items in our bags and in the long term this can damage posture and trigger back and shoulder pain.

57 ON-THE-GO BAGS

Satchels, also known as messenger bags, are ideal for students and travellers as they have long straps so they can be worn across the body, thus leaving the hands free. They are characterized by outer pockets for storing items to which you need easy and quick access.

58 BAG SOME HISTORY

Bags are an easy way to create an era-inspired look. For instance, if you like 1920s style, keep an eye out for dainty beaded bags on long chains, or you could wear a patchwork bag slung across the body to give a relaxed 1970s feel.

59 HOT METAL

A metallic gold or bronze bag looks good in the summer, worn against a white summer dress and a tan.

60 LIFE'S A BEACH

Summer holiday bags should have a relaxed look – but as they will more than likely end up being stained with suntan lotion and grass marks, don't invest a huge amount. Buy cheap bags that are brightly coloured and can hold your book and a beach outfit plus your towel.

61 DON'T ALWAYS GO BACK TO BLACK

Gold and silver metallic bags are a great alternative to classic black as they go with everything and can be worn like jewellery.

62 CARRY A TOTE FOR SHOPPING

Totes and shoppers are great styles for shopping as they have one main compartment for stashing the items that you have bought. Hung from the shoulder, they usually fall at about elbow length. Often made of canvas and open at the top, totes are very large and sturdy. They are also ideal for outdoor activities such as sailing or going to the beach.

63 PRINTS CHARMING

If you feel unsure about wearing prints on your body, you can add this element to your look in the form of a zebra purse or a floral clutch.

64 STAR QUALITY

Bags are a cheap and easy way to introduce a little Hollywood glamour into your look and get on-trend. Keep an eye out in newspapers and magazines for the bags that celebrities are currently wearing, then source similar high-street versions that cost a fraction of the price.

65 VINTAGE FINDS

Check out vintage fairs for one-off styles. Slightly battered leather bags can look fantastic with jeans or slung across a pretty floral summer dress.

66 JOIN THE CHAIN GANG

Look for evening bags with detachable chains or chains that can be tucked neatly inside – then, depending on your outfit, you can wear them on your shoulder or as a clutch bag.

67 ANIMAL MAGIC

For a sophisticated and stylish look, fake crocodile or snakeskin are perfect. Dark red or mustard colours are great alternatives to classic brown and beige.

68 GO HANDS-FREE

If you are a hands-on person who hates the hassle or restrictiveness of carrying a bag, choose a style with a strap that can be worn across the body.

69 STRAP-SAVVY

Before you buy, check the strap of your bag: not only should it be sturdy so that there's no fear of it snapping, but make sure it also stays put on your shoulder.

70 BE SIZE WISE

Make sure you have a variety of different-sized bags to suit every occasion. Plan ahead, too: if you're going out in the evening, downsize by day – you won't want to spend the night lugging around bulky tissues, diary and notebooks in an over-stuffed casual bag.

71 DON'T BE FLASH

Take care when wearing bags with long straps and short skirts – the bag can pull your skirt up as you walk along, displaying more leg than modesty might usually allow!

72 PATENT PRINCESS

For both day and night, patent bags are a great alternative to ordinary leather. They also wear well and can be easily wiped down if they become marked.

73 AVOID SMALL BAGS IF YOU'RE PLUS SIZE

If you are on the large size, avoid small bags and those with short straps, because these will make you look even bigger than you are. Instead, go for a slightly larger and wider style of bag that will balance your look.

74 BAG FOR LIFE

Keep a reusable cloth bag neatly folded inside your handbag at all times. Then, whenever you buy anything, you'll avoid damaging the environment any further as you won't need a plastic bag.

75 MAKE ROOM FOR THE BUCKET

Handbags are designed for certain purposes so know the shapes to look for. Bucket bags, also known as carry-alls, are roomy with short handles, usually open-topped but sometimes closed by a flap. They are a great shape for daily wear as they can hold lots of essentials.

76 BAG A BAG WITH POCKETS

For an organized life, choose an everyday handbag with lots of pockets, compartments and built-in sections for storing your phone, keys, coin purses, diary, sunglasses and other essentials. If you know where to find the items you need, your life will be much more streamlined.

77 CLASSY CLUTCHES

A clutch bag, usually worn in the evening, creates an elegant look. Often called pochettes, the small, envelope-style, understated versions of the clutch are quietly chic, though you may want to try one of the fashionable oversized clutches that grab attention.

jewellery

78 REMEMBER, A GIRL'S BEST FRIEND ...

Diamonds add instant glamour, but don't worry if you can't afford the real thing – costume jewellery looks just as good these days. Layer ropes of pearls around your neck or waist or pin up your hair with a diamanté slide to take a day look effortlessly into the evening.

79 BE A PEARLY QUEEN

Pearl bracelets and necklaces are timeless fashion pieces that sit well against pale floaty fabrics and contrast beautifully with black. Drape long beads around the neck twice and knot in the middle for a more modern twist.

80 WRIST ACTION

The wrists are a very sensual part of the body so don't forget to draw attention to yours. If you have slender wrists, a delicate chain or slim bangle will look great, while chunkier shapes suit larger wrists.

81 JEWELLERY SWAP SHOP

At some stage most of us are given pieces we don't like, only to have them sit at the bottom of our jewellery box. But one person's trash is another's treasure so get together with friends and swap pieces – you're bound to find something each of you prefers.

82 GOLD VERSUS SILVER

The old-fashioned rule is that silver is suitable for dress-down daywear while gold adds extra evening glitz – but actually both can work in either situation. This also depends on your colouring: gold is good for warming up skin tone while silver cools it down. The main thing is to stick to one metal or the other for a more pulled-together look.

83 A NECKLACE FOR ALL SEASONS

Jewellery should go with your outfit but it must also match the season itself. Harder, metallic pieces work well in the winter, while wood and beads are more suited to the summer.

84 COLOURS AND CUFFS

Metal cuffs worn high up the arm are an interesting way to accessorize and look fabulous worn with a maxi dress for a Boho vibe or a Mandarin-collared dress for a hint of Oriental chic.

85 QUANTITY, NOT QUALITY

For a laid-back appearance that's totally up to date, try layering necklaces of different lengths. This works best with thin gold chains – the longer the better.

86 RED, WHITE AND BLUE

Red necklaces look good against white and light blue fabrics. Go for a string of chunky red beads or a simple silver or gold chain with a vivid red pendant such as a heart or cross.

87 GET THE LENGTH RIGHT

Tops with deep or scooped necklines offer a great frame for shorter necklaces while v-necks suit longer pendant necklaces. If your big bust makes you self-conscious, avoid wearing a necklace that nestles into your cleavage and draws attention to it.

89 EASTERN PROMISE

Indian-inspired jewellery is perfect for summer. Team an up-do with bold earrings or stock up on thin, brightly coloured bracelets that you can pick up cheaply in high-street stores. Wear with long skirts and dresses in deep vivid colours for a relaxed Eastern vibe.

90 STYLISH TIMEPIECES

Just because a watch is a practical item, it doesn't need to be dull. Match yours to your style and buy at least two watches – one for day, the other for night. You don't want a chunky day watch to ruin a delicate evening dress, while a fine gold chain can appear out of place with jeans.

91 LET YOUR JEWELLERY DO THE TALKING

If you've splashed out on an expensive piece of jewellery or have even been treated to one, don't let it fight for attention with other pieces. Wear one special piece singly to give it the recognition it deserves.

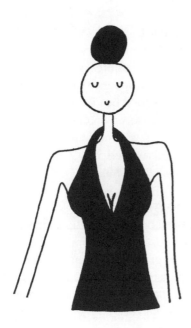

88 HALT STOP!

When wearing halter-neck tops the neck is already a focal point because of the fabric tied around it, so there's no need to add a necklace – it can even look odd. Instead, draw attention to your bare shoulders with a pair of drop or hooped earrings.

92 EVERYDAY ELEGANCE

Just as you have a make-up routine of, say, foundation, mascara and lip gloss, that makes you feel polished and ready to face the world each day, keep a basic jewellery routine for a groomed but understated day look. Choose simple diamond or pearl studs, a favourite ring, single bracelet and classic necklace. You can always vary the look for different outfits and also wear it on the days when you don't want to think about what to wear but still like to look good.

93 FUN AND FUNKY

Have some fun with your fashion and look out for humorous or ironic pieces of jewellery. Necklaces made from scrap metal and funky print scarves all stamp your individuality onto an outfit.

94 GO DANGLE

Just putting your hair up and wearing a pair of glitzy earrings completely changes the tone of an outfit. Hoops and vintage beads will go with most clothes and provide an interesting focal point for otherwise ordinary looks.

95 GO FOR CHOKE

A striking choker necklace worn with a strapless top or dress breaks up an outfit and adds extra glamour to the bare skin on show. Look for a beaded style of necklace that picks up on one or more of the colours in your outfit, or add sparkle to a black dress with Audrey Hepburn-style diamanté.

96 PIN IT TOGETHER

A well-placed brooch livens up a little black dress and adds a splash of instant colour to your coat or sweater. Keep an eye out for vintage cameos or jewelled brooches in interesting shapes in second-hand stores and antique markets.

97 HEART ON YOUR SLEEVE

Charm bracelets are always in vogue. Not only are they a great fashion accessory that goes with anything, but they also allow you to carry memories around on your wrist. Plus any unusual charm tends to be attention-grabbing and makes a great conversation-starter at parties.

98 LAYER BANGLES

Adding a few bangles instantly livens up an outfit and there are hundreds of different styles out there to choose from. Look for bangles made of wood or bright Perspex – it's all about being bold and stacking them up.

99 ROCK ON

Thanks to costume jewellery, it's now perfectly possible to wear a big rock on your finger for a fraction of the cost. Keep a selection of rings with different coloured stones and metals to match different outfits.

scarves, wraps & belts

100 FAKE IT

For a classy 1950s evening look, try a fake-fur stole. Go for simple black, white or cream with a ribbon attached that you can throw around your shoulders and tie in a bow at your chest or neck.

101 SCARF CHIC

You can never have too many scarves in all colours and sizes. Chiffon ones are particularly useful as they add sophistication when worn as a little shawl over a strapless evening dress or as a neck scarf with a plain shirt, and can even be tied around a straw hat to coordinate a wedding outfit.

102 SNUGGLE UP IN STYLE

Woolly scarves keep you warm and look great, too. Treat yourself to ones you love in soft fabrics and pretty colours and patterns. The winter months are long and you'll wear them often, so have a few scarves to tie in with different coats.

103 ORGANIZE YOUR ACCESSORIES

If you have the wardrobe space, invest in a
scarf hanger, which has holes for the scarves
to pull through. Your scarves will never be
creased again and the hanger can be used
for everything from silk scarves to pashminas.
A belt hanger is also a good idea so that you
can easily see and choose the item you want
for your outfit. Make sure you buy one that
enables you to take off items and replace
them one by one rather than a hoop style.

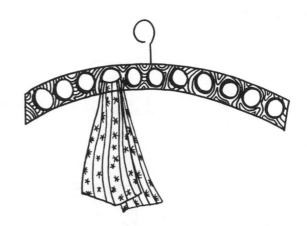

104 WRAP IT UP

Invest in a few plain-coloured silk and
wool pashminas. They look far better
over evening dresses than cardigans
or jackets and add instant chic to a
simple jeans-and-top combo.

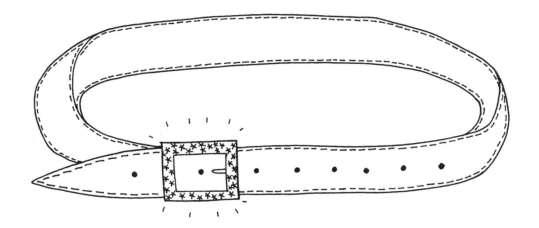

other accessories

105 BELT IT

Belts are an instant way to add glamour to a plain outfit or dress, so look for styles that have interesting or intricate detailing. Belts can also provide a more affordable way of wearing designer items – and another advantage is that they will last for years.

106 UNDER THE WEATHER

Keep dry and look fashionable by buying a stylish umbrella. Forget boring black and instead look for bright colours and patterns that will help brighten up your mood and raise your umbrella from practical item to fashion statement.

108 GLAMOROUS GLOVES

There are so many different styles of glove in every fabric and colour, so there's no excuse not to have a pair to match every outfit. Choose jewelled or sequined detail for eveningwear, or try mittens for a cute daytime alternative – they are perfect for long winter walks.

107 ADD A HAT

Nothing attracts attention quite like a hat. It takes confidence to wear one so choose classic shapes such as a fedora or beret to make the look easier to pull off.

109 USE YOUR HEAD

Not everyone suits the same shape of hat so choose carefully. Knitted berets look good with hair tucked up inside or with short styles, while 'beanies' suit wearers with long sleek hair. Wide brims are good for larger heads and neat pillar-box styles are perfect for smaller heads.

110 PICK THE RIGHT SHADES

Perhaps the most versatile item you can own is a great pair of sunglasses. They add an air of mystery and can look stylish when worn on top of your head. Keep a few pairs of sunglasses including oversized and vintage so that you have something to suit every occasion.

111 HAIR TO THE THRONE

Hair slides and grips are necessities when it comes to keeping hair out of your face, but they also provide a great way to dress up an outfit. Jewelled styles are fabulous for day or night, and it's also worth learning how to use special ties and combs for chignons and plaits (braids).

112 OPTICAL STYLE

If you wear glasses, it's worth spending the time and effort to choose the shape and colour of your frames – the right pair can cross the divide from functional to fashion statement. Most opticians offer a service where you can have photos taken so that you can check your overall look. Many stores also have specially trained advisors who can take you through the best colours and shapes for your face and prescription.

113 ALICE IN WONDERBANDS

Alice bands have come a long way since the 1980s Sloane Ranger days. Thick fabric ones look great whatever your hair length, and in emergencies they can be used to cover a multitude of sins from bad roots to greasy day-before-washing locks.

adding a personal touch

114 BE DARING

Don't rule out accessories on the basis that you've never worn them before or they're 'just not me'. Keep experimenting with new things. If you change your hair colour or length, different accessories previously dismissed – such as large earrings, chokers or scarves – may now work.

115 SAY IT WITH FLOWERS

For an instant update, attach big fabric flowers to straw hats, hair bands, bracelets or brooches for a soft, feminine look that's perfect for summer days.

116 BREATHE NEW LIFE INTO OLD OUTFITS

Cash-flow crisis? Before you buy a new outfit for a special occasion, see if an existing favourite can be dressed up with funky accessories. A cool hat or striking choker may be all that is needed.

117 GET CREATIVE

Break up a plain outfit by tying a pretty scarf around your waist as a belt, or try using clip-on earrings to jazz up a pair of court shoes. You could also tie a scarf around your hair with the tails hanging underneath to one side for a sophisticated Parisian look.

118 BEAD IT

Adding a flash of beads will jazz up the dullest outfit. Invest in a few beaded or sequined accessories – such as purses, belts and necklaces – and keep them in your drawer at work to add sparkle in case you are invited out for impromptu after-work drinks.

119 STOCK UP ON SNIPPETS

Your accessory drawer is your box of tricks when it comes to updating your look or transforming an otherwise dull outfit. Keep it stocked with plenty of inexpensive belts, scarves and jewellery, adding a few new pieces each season so that you always look up-to-the-minute.

120 PLAY UP THE POSITIVES

Use accessories to draw attention to a part of your body that you like, such as a pair of sapphire earrings to accentuate your blue eyes or a cinched-in belt to show off your tiny waist.

121 A BIT OF BLING

Use statement accessories to bring a plain outfit to life. For example, team intricate diamanté earrings or belts with streamlined, simple black dresses or jeans.

122 KEEP IT SIMPLE

Never over-accessorize. Wearing killer heels, a big necklace and a flashy belt at the same time can make an outfit confusing. For maximum impact, stick with just one or two key items at a time.

123 TAKE A BOW

Keep the pieces of ribbon that you receive on gifts to jazz up bags, belts or even shoes, choosing colours that tie in with your outfit.

colour coding

124 THE COLOUR TEST

Different colours suit different women – it depends on whether your skin has a cool or warm undertone. To find out, hold a piece of plain white paper under your hand and look closely at the colour of your skin. If the overall hue of your hand is blue-ish, you have a cool skin tone, while if you see yellow, you have a warm skin tone.

125 WARM UNDERTONE

If you have a warm skin undertone, the best colours to flatter your complexion are earthy tones – browns, beige, olive, peach, corals and gold or yellows.

126 COOL UNDERTONE

If you have a cool skin undertone – which means a pink or rosy tone, you will look best in colours from the blue, green and purple family – shades such as pale blue, rose pink and purple.

127 GOLD OR SILVER?

If you have a warm complexion, silver can look stunning, while gold will warm up cooler skin tones. To find out which one works for you, hold a piece of gold fabric up next to your face and then swap it for silver and see which colour makes your face look brighter.

128 COLOURS TO SUIT ALL

There are some colours that work on nearly all complexions because they fall in the middle of the colour spectrum. Aubergine, purple, darker red, teal and light peachy pink are all safe shades for different complexions to wear.

129 LOOK INTO YOUR EYES

In theory, the greater the contrast between your eyes, skin and hair colour, the bolder the colours you can get away with wearing. If, for example, you have olive skin but blonde hair and brown eyes, bright exotic shades will suit you. Pale skin, hair and eyes suit more pastel hues.

130 DON'T BE AFRAID TO COPY

One of the many reasons why celebrities always look good is because they wear clothes in colours to suit their complexions. Look in magazines for photos of famous women who have the same colouring as you and take note of the colours and shades they wear.

131 PORCELAIN DOLLS

If you have a porcelain skin colour like Nicole Kidman, soft tans, greens and lavenders are perfect to flatter your pale skin tone.

132 SUMMER TIME

Women who have 'summer' colouring will have grey-blue eyes mixed in with some hazel or green colourings and their hair is often dark blonde or brunette. They look great in denim and neutral colours such as cream, tan and navy. For a splash of colour, summer types should wear pastel colours such as pale mint, dusky raspberry and pinks.

133 WINTER WONDERS

Women with dark brown to black hair, dark brown or green eyes, and olive skin are likely to fall into the 'winter' category. For neutral clothes, look for items in black, charcoal grey and dark navy; for colour, winters look great in regal purples, emerald green, magenta and burgundy.

134 ORIENTAL STYLE

Women with oriental skin have a slightly peachy tone to their colouring and look great in white clothes. Pale colours also work well but women of this skin type can achieve an instant sophisticated look by wearing black.

135 AUTUMN BEAUTY

If you are an 'autumn' woman, you will match the colour of the season with bronze, copper or ginger hair and warm, golden skin undertones. You may have very pale skin with freckles. Flame red, gold, deep teal, dark orange and olive colours work best for autumns. For neutral shades, try khaki, coffee and cream tones.

136 STEP INTO SPRING

Women with 'spring' colouring are recognizable for a peaches-and-cream complexion that tans easily. Their eyes tend to be light and their hair colour is often wheat, strawberry blonde or brown. The best shades to wear are those that mirror the season, such as peach, apricot and sunny yellows, light blue, plus bright aqua and turquoise.

137 FACE-TO-FACE

Since the colour of the skin on your face shows your true skin tone, for maximum impact make sure you always wear the colours that suit you best closest to your face. If you want to wear a shade that isn't in your palette, position this further away – try a skirt, shoes or handbag.

138 BREAK THE RULES

Of course you can still wear colours that are not in your seasonal colourings as long as you always team them with one of the shades that you know works best with your skin tone.

139 SAY NO TO SHADE, NOT COLOUR

No colour has to be out of bounds because of your hair and skin tone – just certain shades of that colour. As a basic rule, the lightest pastel shade of a colour will suit those with a summer complexion, while the darkest shades will look best on winter women. For example, a light blue will suit a summer and a royal blue or midnight would work better for a winter.

140 FOLLOW YOUR INSTINCTS

We are often subconsciously led to choose the colours that suit us best so follow your instincts on colour when out shopping. Look at old photographs to see what colours you look best in and bear them in mind when choosing new clothes.

141 BACK TO BLACK

Not just for funerals, head-to-toe black is universally accepted as chic. It's a flattering uniform that can be worn day or night and suits almost every occasion, but don't wear it every day or it does become a little boring.

capsule collection

142 STAY NEUTRAL

A capsule wardrobe full of neutral shades can reduce the amount of time you have to spend putting looks together because you already have basics that work together. Keep to black, navy, grey, beige, cream and white.

143 CHOOSE ANY COLOUR ...

So long as it's black! Black is a fail-safe colour that never goes out of fashion. Staple blacks should form the basis of any capsule wardrobe, so make sure you have a good strong collection of classic trousers, jackets, skirts, dresses and tops in different weights of fabric.

144 ACCESSORIZE YOUR CLASSICS

Each item in your capsule wardrobe should be a classic fit that can be worn year after year and accessorized or lifted with on-trend items. Choose cheaper items such as blouses and fashionable skirts to add each season, which will introduce pattern and colour.

145 LESS QUANTITY, MORE QUALITY

The idea behind the capsule wardrobe
is to have fewer items but have them
of high quality, so that they last longer
and look chic.

146 BASIC ELEMENTS

Paring your wardrobe down to a capsule
collection allows you to have high-
functioning clothes that perform many
different uses. Even just two pairs of
black trousers can take you from the
office to the evening most days of the
week. Other staples include a white fitted
shirt and a pencil skirt. Aim to have at
least two pairs of trousers and two skirts
– one dark, one light – two plain shirts,
two simple tops and a good jacket. They
should all be in solid neutral colours.

147 A GROOMED SILHOUETTE

Consider shape, too, when shopping
for your capsule wardrobe. Aim for a
streamlined silhouette, which works for
all body shapes and will enable you to
use layering without creating bulk.

capsule accessories

148 THE RIGHT BOX OF TRICKS

A capsule wardrobe should exude groomed put-together style, so don't ruin it by throwing on any old piece of jewellery. Make sure accessories complement not just your outfit but each other, too. One long and one short simple necklace are must-haves.

149 STYLISH SUNGLASSES

For real glamour, pick up a stylish pair of sunglasses. Take a friend with you when looking for the right pair and try on as many shapes and styles as you can so that you find the perfect sunglasses for your face shape.

150 MAN-SIZE

Women's watches tend to change according to trends but a classic man's watch is timeless and also looks great on a woman's wrist. It makes a statement and breaks the rules in an unexpected but stylish way.

151 A PASSION FOR PASHMINAS

With so many uses, a pashmina or two should be found in every woman's wardrobe. Wear them as a shawl over bare arms in the summer and around the neck in winter. They can bring an outfit alive, so look out for ones featuring interesting detailing.

152 THE ULTIMATE LEATHER HANDBAG

A well-made classic leather bag will last you for years and instantly adds style and sophistication to your look. Perfect for work, interviews and meetings, it's worth investing a bit more in a great bag – and with leather you get what you pay for.

153 HIGHS AND LOWS

The right shoes can make or break an outfit so you should spend time choosing a pair that will last and may be worn with a variety of clothes. A well-made pair of pumps in a subtle colour can be worn to work and will also keep a weekend style looking smart. Every woman also needs a pair of killer heels to wear on nights out.

154 BE A BELTER

With a capsule wardrobe, accessories such as belts are the perfect way to update old looks. Make sure you have a dressy belt that you can team with dresses or skirts, a brown leather style to wear with jeans, and a slouchy belt for around the hips.

155 STICK THE BOOT IN

Finding the right boot to flatter your leg and suit your style can take time – but persevere. A smart pair of knee-high boots should be an important part of your winter wardrobe as they look great with skirts and dresses and suit almost all legs shapes, as they hide chunky calves and ankles.

156 SMART WITH A SCARF

A square silk scarf is indispensable (Grace Kelly used her Hermès scarf as a sling for a broken arm!). It can jazz up any outfit, from a little black dress to a business suit or jeans and a jacket. It can be worn as a belt, halter-top, sarong, as a shawl over a jacket, on the head, or to accent a handbag. Or tie it round the neck!

157 TIGHT FIT

Even if you love coloured tights, make sure that you always have handy two pairs of good-quality black tights and two pairs of skin-colour tights in your underwear drawer – one or the other will go with every outfit.

basic knitwear essentials

158 CLASSY CASHMERE

Although expensive, a cashmere sweater will hold its shape, feel amazing and never go out of style. It is super-soft, lightweight and offers 'breathability'. The highest class of natural fibre (from Kashmir goats), cashmere can be worn with smart trousers or jeans and works well in both summer and winter. The number of times you will end up wearing the sweater means that its cost per wear makes it a worthwhile investment.

159 COOL CARDIE

Easy to wear and suitable for both the office and weekends, a fitted, well-made cardigan takes some beating for versatility. Go for a neutral shade that you can team with an array of outfits. Make sure it's a good-quality garment that won't lose its shape over time.

160 FANTASTIC FABRIC

Go for a fine-wool knit jumper (sweater) and keep the shape tailored but simple. Merino is durable, soft and resistant to creasing and wear. Don't be tempted to go for the latest fur trim or funnel neck shape – it will look dated by next year. Stick to a classic design and you can wear it year after year with different scarves and gloves.

161 WOOL WORKS

Through the cold winter months, a good-quality, chunky-knit top will keep you looking warm and fashionable. A big-knit long cardigan with a waist belt is a classic buy that defines your shape so you don't look too bulky.

basic shirts & tops

162 NECK IT

When it comes to tops and sweaters, it's good to have an assortment of necklines to match with different jackets and a cardie. Ensure you have at least two v-necks, two scoop necks and two polo necks – all in neutral shades.

163 VESTS FOR LAYERING

Spaghetti-strap vests in black, beige, cream and navy are useful to layer under jackets and transparent shirts. As they are inexpensive, they can be renewed frequently. Keep an eye out for sales to stock up on coloured versions, too.

164 THE CLASSIC WHITE SHIRT

A tailored shirt will look great for work and can also be dressed down with jeans at the weekend. Choose good-quality cotton for crispness.

165 TOP IT OFF

Have at least two sexy party tops in your wardrobe that will flatter your figure and are versatile. Look out for a pretty camisole and a sequined top – one in a light shade and the other dark. The idea is that they look good with both skirts and trousers and can be smartened up or dressed down depending on the occasion.

166 SHOP FOR TOPS

Fitted T-shirts and vests in a wide variety of colours are the staples of any versatile wardrobe. For a great shape, choose fabrics with a hint of stretch – but not too much or they will cling to lumps and bumps. A ribbed white-and-black vest top goes with everything and can be worn alone or under other tops and dresses.

167 SOFTLY SOFTLY

A floaty chiffon blouse that can be teamed with capsule skirts or trousers can add femininity to a sharp-tailored look and break up a hard silhouette. Choose ones that are lined to avoid the see-through problem.

skirts & dresses

168 DRESS TO IMPRESS

An easy day-to-evening dress is simple to
pull off and requires no thinking – you
can concentrate on the accessories you'll
wear with it rather than worry if the top
works with the skirt or trousers. Look for
something with classic lines that will show
off your best features, whether that's your
legs, bust or waistline.

169 LOOK FOR AN LBD

A little black dress is an essential that's
worth spending a bit of money on. Look for
a design that is simple and well cut and can
be worn during the day with a blazer over
the top or jazzed up with jewellery and glitzy
shoes at night.

170 SUMMER LOVING

A pretty summer dress is a must-have.
Choose one that can be worn for both
day and evening summer events. Floral is
timeless, while block colours can date.

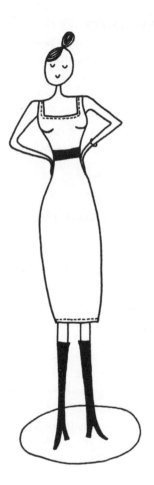

171 SKIRT THE SUBJECT

When you have the choice between wearing trousers or a skirt, carefully weigh up your options – and then choose the skirt. It's so much easier to find a skirt that suits you, whereas with trousers you have to consider the rise, the width of the hips, the legs and how it falls across your bottom.

172 FLIRTY SKIRTY

A full knee-length skirt looks great in summer and is the perfect way to incorporate some pattern or print into your wardrobe. Choose a satin or silk pleated skirt for instant Parisian chic.

173 DAY AND NIGHT

A dark knee-length skirt is an essential. Skinny girls should choose A-line shapes while pencil skirts suit those with curvier figures. A simple skirt like this can be worn with a plain fitted top or shirt for daytime and then vamped up with a sexy, shimmery top for the evening.

174 DRESS ME DOWN

Smart enough for work but laidback enough for weekends and holidays, a great shirtdress is always an investment buy. For maximum versatility, keep it fitted and in a subtle colour.

175 VERSATILE DENIM

A classic denim skirt is ideal for casual urban style, but choosing the correct length and weight of fabric is essential. An A-line that falls to the knee, which is in a soft lightweight denim, can be worn with a variety of shoes and dressed up or down.

coats & jackets

176 THE SCRUNCH TEST

Always check the crumple potential of any coat. Grab a handful of fabric and squeeze it hard for ten seconds. If it looks crumpled, so will you.

177 GET INTO A TRENCH

A well-fitting trench coat is smart enough to wear to work, but also perfect when teamed with jeans for a stylish weekend look. Go for a light-coloured one as a contrast to your dark winter coat.

178 CHECK THE FIT

The mark of a coat that fits well is that you can cross your arms in front of you and still reach up comfortably. Make sure the coat tapers in at the waist, fits snugly on the shoulders and that the sleeves aren't below the middle of your thumb in length.

179 WINTER WEAR

A good winter coat is one of the most important items you will buy, so spend time getting the right one. Remember, you will be wearing it most days so it needs to be versatile – a mid-length works for most needs. Avoid boxy styles, which can look frumpy, and choose one with a shaped waist that will suit all figures. A dark wool or cashmere blend will last year after year.

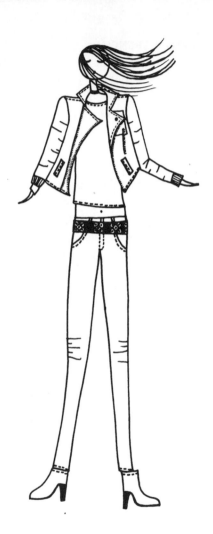

180 BAG A BLAZER

Make sure you have a good-fitting blazer, either in wool, cord or velvet. It's so versatile you will be able to team it with everything from dresses to skirts and jeans for a smart-casual look.

181 BAG A BIKER

The shrunken black leather biker jacket, like the close-fitting denim jacket, is a favourite that never goes far out of fashion. Worn mostly with skinny jeans by the fashion pack, it is useful to add a punk feel to an outfit. Alternatively, pair it with tailored trousers for an androgynous look or with a body-conscious jersey dress.

182 BEST BLAZER

A structured jacket can be thrown over trousers, skirts, dresses and jeans and can add instant shape to an outfit. It should skim over your flaws and make you feel more pulled-together, taller and sleeker. Single-breasted flatter the most shapes and the best styles are those that define the shoulders and waist.

trousers & suits

183 LOOSE-FIT TROUSERS

Loose-fit trousers, à la Kate Hepburn, should be worn with a tight shirt to balance out the volume. Loose worn with loose looks sloppy, and tight on tight can look trashy. Tailored classic neutral-coloured trousers with a turn-up (cuff) look especially smart.

184 DREAM DENIM

Jeans are a key staple. A well-cut pair can be dressed up or down depending on the occasion. It's a good idea to have at least two pairs of well-fitting jeans – one pair in a darker shade for winter and a second pair in a lighter colour for summer.

185 WEAR THE TROUSERS

Every wardrobe needs at least two pairs of smart trousers that fit perfectly, can be worn with anything and make you feel great when you put them on. Tailored wide-cut or bootcut shapes tend to flatter everyone and can be dressed up or down.

186 LOVELY LINEN

A flattering pair of linen trousers is key to your wardrobe. By choosing a pair in a neutral shade you'll look perfect during those tricky transitional months between summer and winter. Choose beige rather than white as the trousers will stay looking smarter for longer and show less dirt.

187 KEEP THE SHAPE

Choose robust fabrics such as wool crepe, wool gabardine or stretch blends for trousers and suits if you want them to keep their shape long-term. Heavier fabric also hangs better and won't cling to lumps and bumps. Wool is the best option for cool-weather suits and trousers but make sure the garment is fully lined.

188 CHECK THE POCKETS

Pay particular attention to the placement of pockets and any detailing on them. Pockets on the rear of trousers should be placed high to keep the bottom looking pert, not stretched down the thighs, which will drag the bottom down and shorten the leg.

189 SUITED SEPARATES

For a great-fitting suit, choose a label that offers separates so you can choose a different fit for the jacket and trousers. Many women are a different size top and bottom and it is rare that an off-the-peg suit will fit perfectly.

190 SLIM SHADING FOR SUITS

If you own one suit it should be in a dark colour in order to create a slim, long line. The suit can be accented with a colourful scarf, shirt, handbag or shoes. If you find black too harsh for your colouring or complexion, or you live in a hot climate where it looks very dense, choose a charcoal, beige or navy suit as your staple.

191 SUIT IT UP

A well-cut trouser suit is one of the best items you can buy for your capsule wardrobe. The trousers should be straight-cut or bootleg, with flat fronts (no pleats) and enough stretch for comfort. Pockets on the jacket or trousers should be without flaps to keep the look streamlined.

192 PIN YOUR HOPES ON PINSTRIPES

The menswear-inspired pinstripe works beautifully on women, either for the office or for a casual look. For your classic capsule wardrobe, choose a navy or black narrow-pinstripe trouser, which can be mixed-and-matched with other neutrals. Add a feminine detail like a ribbon belt to soften the look.

finding the perfect jeans

193 JEAN-IUS!

Often people don't realize that a good tailor can alter jeans to give a perfect fit. Jeans that fit in the leg but are too big in the waist can be taken in while panels may be added to the sides of jeans for extra room. If they're too long in the leg, it's well worth paying to have your jeans taken up. Not only will they look better, they'll also last longer as you won't be constantly treading on the hems.

194 SKINNY WITH STYLE

Though skinny jeans refuse to go away, they can be hard to pull off. Wear them with a good pair of heels; flat ballet pumps are a popular choice but they make even the slinkiest celebrities seem larger-hipped.

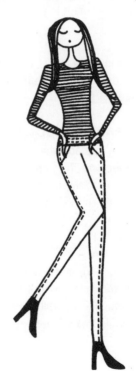

195 THE HIPS DON'T LIE

Fact: Many women are pear-shaped – especially in the West – and hipster jeans are the most flattering for this figure. They'll make your bottom look small, your waist tiny and, if worn with heels, they'll give you long and elegant legs.

186 GO LOW

When trying on low-rise jeans, sit down in them first to check that everything remains covered at the back!

197 IF IN DOUBT, BANK ON BOOTCUT

Bootcut jeans are arguably the most flattering for everyone. They create the overall impression of length, they slim the thighs, balance thick calves and make ankles look delicate.

198 LOVE YOUR LYCRA

If you're apple-shaped, go for jeans with a bit of added stretch as this will help slim your tummy area. Slim-fits will flatter your small bottom while low-waisters disguise a thick waistline.

199 FITTED, NOT FRUMPY

If you're petite, choose a fitted pair of jeans instead of baggy boyfriend cuts that will swamp you and make you look even smaller than you are.

200 BUY IN PAIRS

Finding the perfect pair of jeans is no easy feat so when you discover the right style for you, buy two pairs. When one falls into disrepair, you won't be devastated if you find they've been discontinued.

201 THE BOTTOM LINE ON POCKETS

The size of back pockets on jeans is crucial to how they will make your bottom look, so go for medium to large pockets that slim and shape your behind. Avoid small pockets or jeans with no back pockets at all as they will make your backside look bigger.

202 BOTTOMS UP

Low-rise jeans with a wide waistband also give the illusion of a neat, rounder behind because they make the material around the butt area appear smaller.

203 HOW TO WEAR YOUR JEANS

Jeans can be worn with heels, tucked into boots, with ballet pumps or with trainers. When shopping for jeans, consider which type of footwear you plan to wear with your jeans as it will influence the length and the shape. Skinny jeans look great tucked into boots, for example, but boy-fit slouchy ones don't!

204 EARNING THEIR KEEP

Jeans are probably the hardest-working item in your wardrobe so it's worth spending a bit of time to work out what style best suits your figure before you part with your hard-earned cash. Visit your nearest department store or jeans specialist to try on the 10–15 pairs you like to discover what does – and doesn't – suit you.

205 LEG LENGTHENER

If you have a long back and shorter legs, avoid very low-rise jeans as they will make your upper body look longer still. Go for high-waisted styles and team with a top that just skims your hips.

206 YEEE HA!

Unless you want to look like a country and western singer, don't wear a matching denim jacket and jeans – it just looks tacky! Save the jacket for non-denim but casual trousers or skirts, and wear a cotton jacket, trench or a long cardigan with jeans for a more casual look.

207 LONG TALL SALLY

If you're tall, you can get away with pretty much any shape or style of jeans. Show off your long pins with low-rise, straight-legged styles and roll up the bottoms in summer for a casual look. Look out for extra-long versions of standard jeans now made by most manufacturers.

208 BE INDIVIDUAL

Personalized jeans, using embroidery, studs or rhinestones to add glamour, can look fantastic. If you're heavy round the hips, make use of pretty detailing around the lower part of jeans to draw the eye away from problem areas. Don't overdo it, though – subtlety is key.

209 ONE OF THE BOYS

Man-shaped jeans can be very flattering if they're worn right. They also tend to be cut more generously on the thighs. Straight-legged medium-width jeans that sit just below the natural waist exude a 1970s vibe when worn with a white ruffled blouse and high heels.

210 GET A GOOD FIT

Don't buy jeans just because the size on the label looks good. Sizes and cuts vary widely between brands so start with your normal size but don't be reluctant to choose the next size up if they don't feel good. A comfortable pair of jeans that fits well will always look good.

211 DON'T LET THEM FADE AWAY

The best way to keep dark indigo colours vivid is to wash them in cold water with only a little detergent and to dry them indoors rather than on a line outside where they can be faded by the sun. Iron your jeans inside out to avoid leaving any shiny scorch marks.

212 GIVING RISE?

Jeans have become lower and lower over the past few years but unless you're ultra-skinny with a perfectly flat stomach, avoid super low-risers – instead, choose styles that sit on or above the hips. To check the fit, use the three-finger rule: place three fingers just below your tummy button. The lowest waist you should go for should have this spacing.

213 JEANS TLC

Most denim specialists advise leaving jeans well alone. Washing them too often causes fading and wear and tear, so only wash them when it's really necessary. Denim is a hardwearing fabric that doesn't get dirty or start to smell easily. If you can't bear to leave your jeans, make sure that when you do wash them you choose a cool cycle and they are turned inside out.

214 THE DARKER, THE BETTER

Unless you're ultra-thin, stay away from very light-coloured or stonewashed jeans. Dark jeans make everyone look slimmer and will go with just about anything.

215 THE LONGER, THE BETTER

When you go shopping, wear a pair of shoes with heels similar to those you usually wear with jeans. Keep in mind that when jeans shrink, so too can the length, which means it's better to go for the longer pair.

216 CARE WITH FLARES

Stay away from large flared legs – they only add bulk. Your jeans should have just the right amount of curve at the bottom of the legs to look stylish and make your legs appear longer.

217 EMPTY YOUR POCKETS

Remember, jeans pockets were designed for looks, not practicality. Don't stuff them with tissues, spare lipgloss, loose change and so on – it will spoil the line and you'll also appear rumpled.

lovely lingerie

218 AVOID BACK PROBLEMS

A poorly fitted bra can not only be unsightly under clothes but also can be unhealthy. If the bust is not well supported, the breasts will fall to the bottom of the cup and put extra strain on the shoulders and neck to support the weight of the breasts. An underwired bra provides extra support underneath the bust.

219 CHECK THE SIZE

To make sure your bra fits correctly, your finger should be able to pass underneath the band at the front, and the middle of the bra should lie flat against your breastbone. If the back of the bra rides up, you probably need a smaller size; if your breasts squeeze over the top of the cups, but all else feels fine, then you need a bigger cup size. The straps should not dig in or fall off the shoulder – make sure you have adjustable straps so that you can alter the fit.

220 MATCHING PAIRS

Feel fashionable from the skin layer up by always wearing matching bras and panties if you can. Buy lingerie in sets, with extra knickers, so that you look as groomed underneath as you do to the public.

221 ALL CHANGE

Don't wear the same bra in your forties as you did in your twenties. Your shape may have changed, plus bra technology nowadays can make you look trimmer and perter than ever before.

222 CAMISOLES

Double up a lacy lingerie-
type silk camisole as a sexy
summer top. This works if
you team it with something
more masculine, such as boy
jeans or a trousersuit but
never wear it with a silky skirt
or soft unstructured trousers,
which will look as if you
belong in the bedroom. Layer
two similar ones together
for more coverage if you're
worried and always wear a
strapless smooth-cupped bra
underneath. If you're on the
busty side, this is probably not
the best daytime look for you
as you'll need more coverage.

223 CALL IN THE PROFESSIONALS

Always wear a professionally fitted bra. Have your bust measured at your local department store or underwear shop to ensure a perfect fit. A recent survey found that 60% of women were wearing the wrong size bra.

224 LOOK FOR A MULTIWAY

Most brands do a bra that can be worn in a variety of ways with detachable straps and extra eyelets and buttons. There is even one that claims to be able to be worn 100 different ways, so there's no excuse for not wearing a bra under your clothes, no matter how revealing they are.

225 STAY IN SHAPE WITH SPORTS BRAS

Sports bras are specifically designed to help reduce bounce and provide extra support when performing athletic activities. Although 77% of women don't wear one, preferring ordinary bras or a crop top, breast movement during sport strains the ligaments that hold the breast in place, causing them to stretch and leading to long-term sagging.

226 AVOID THE PINCH

Take a good look at the bras you wear every day and consider whether they truly fit you as well as they could. A good bra gives you a continuous smooth line and should not create any bulges under the arms, across the back, under the breast or across the cleavage.

227 BIG BOSOMS

Large-breasted women should always get a professional fit; a good bra will lift the breasts and define the waist, plus provide support for heavy breasts. A thick band rather than an underwire often provides better support. A minimizer bra can be a good choice under suits.

228 BALCONY BRAS FOR SMALLER BREASTS

A balcony bra can give you an enhanced neckline, excellent uplift, and a lovely, curvy shape. Half-cup bras also flatter a smaller bust; padding at the sides and under the bust give maximum lift. Avoid bras that have square-cut bust lines; they'll flatten you even more.

229 BE A SMOOTHIE

Invest in some smooth, well-shaped underwear that fits perfectly. Good panties should hold in any lumps and help improve your posture. Power panties like Spanx create a smooth line and are super slimming – they also carry further down the leg to tighten the whole area while still feeling sexy.

230 KNOW YOUR CUP SIZE

Measure your chest just under the breasts. If the number is even, add 4 inches; if the number is odd, add 5 inches. Now measure the fullest width across your breasts. If the numbers are the same you are an A cup; if 1 inch more, a B; if 2 inches more, a C; if 3 inches more, a D; if 4 inches more a DD.

231 MATCH YOUR BRA TO YOUR CLOTHES

Different bras provide different functions. For a streamlined look under tailored office clothes, wear a bra with a bit of uplift and firmer support. For casual wear, you may prefer a softer seamless bra to go under clingy tops and T-shirts. If your weight varies due to hormone fluctuations throughout the month, choose a bra with some Lycra, which will adjust more readily to the changes.

232 GIVE SLIPS THE SLIP

Forget wearing a slip. These days underwear is so invisible there's no point in adding the extra bulk and folds – plus it can look really tacky if it shows below your hemline.

233 REAR VIEW MIRROR

Always check out your back view in a full-length mirror before you go out, watching out for VPL or other unsightly bumps and bulges. Remember that your rear view is 50% of what people see – which is a big percentage!

234 DROOPY DRAWERS

It's easy to make the mistake of thinking you can get away with wearing any old shabby underwear simply because it's hidden from sight – and especially when you're in a hurry to get ready in the morning. In fact, badly fitting bras and panties ruin the whole shape and line of even the most expensive outfit, so make sure you plan your underwear as well.

235 CREATE AN UNDIES WARDROBE

Make sure you have a good range of different bras to suit the various necklines and backs of the clothes in your wardrobe. A strapless, a halterneck and a backless bra should cover most dress shapes. Keep a selection of panties that match.

236 EASY RIDER

Ditch any bra that rides up at the back – this suggests it is too big, which means your boobs are getting no support.

237 UP CLOSE AND PERSONAL

Even if you're in great shape, some clothes just need a layer between you and the fabric – this is especially so with any sort of seamed garment intended to show off the line of your body. It might feel a bit 1950s, but the right underwear can make all the difference to your outfit, so don't go commando!

238 FLESH IT OUT

White underwear will show through sheer summer clothes. Unless this is intentional (and if you're not Madonna, it shouldn't be), choose the correct colour bra and pants. The key is to wear undies in flesh tones that match the colour of your skin, not the outfit. If in doubt, they should be one shade darker than your skin. Try to shop wearing neutral underwear so you can see exactly how a sheer item will look.

beachwear

239 TALL AND SHORT OF IT

If you're tall, to avoid looking like a beanpole on the beach, don't go for up-and-down stripes, high necklines or solid block colours. Tall women can carry off brightly coloured swimwear, and bikini shorts are perfect for slim hips. If you prefer wearing all-in-ones to bikinis, look out for waist detail or belts on bikini bottoms to give your body more waist definition.

240 HIP-SWINGING

Pear shapes should wear a darker bottom and a brighter top to draw attention away from their bigger bottom half. High-cut bikini bottoms make your butt look smaller and your legs longer.

241 LITTLE UP TOP

If you are small on top, look for bikini tops that have built-in padding or underwiring. Details such as ruffles or prints will create the illusion of curves.

242 HIGH THIGH

If you have short legs or a stubby torso, go for swimwear that's cut high on the thigh as this will make your legs look longer. Don't be tempted to go for bikini shorts because they draw the eye downward and make you look shorter than you are.

243 INVEST IN THE BEST

You never show off your body more than on the beach or by the pool, so do it justice by buying a really well-fitting, flattering swimsuit. All-in-one pieces and bikinis alike should give firm, uplifting support and hold you in, in all the right places. For the top, make sure you consider all the factors you would when buying a bra.

244 FOR SHOW, NOT SWIM

If you are planning a trip where you will be posing (say, on a yacht!) rather than swimming, you can choose a swimsuit with 'hardware' such as jewelled pieces and chains. Otherwise, avoid the bling, as these glitzy details shouldn't come in contact with too much water!

245 HALTER EGO

For those with bigger busts, halter-neck top bikinis not only offer support but create enviable cleavage, too. Go for tops that provide some support and have thicker straps – they will be more comfortable. And look for one-piece swimsuits with built-in structure such as soft foam cups.

246 ACTIVE GIRLS

You If you are an active swimmer or surfer, choose your beachwear accordingly, as you'll only be disappointed if it doesn't perform. Choose a snug swimsuit in a thicker, more durable nylon or spandex; racer-back styles and halters maximize the range of your shoulder motions. Or try boardshorts, which are lightweight, fast-drying and stretchy.

247 PATTERN PRINCIPLES

Patterns on swimsuits can have the effect of making the eye concentrate on the pattern instead of what lurks behind it! Choose the pattern depending on your shape. The smaller you are, the smaller the pattern you can get away with, but on a fuller figure a small and delicate pattern will enhance your size, so go for a larger and bolder pattern that your body can carry off.

248 PERFECT COVER

Sarongs can cover a multitude of sins on the beach, so be stylish and find one that matches your swimsuit or bikini perfectly.

249 CHOOSE A BIKINI FOR YOUR BODY

There are almost as many styles of bikinis as figures to fit them. Look at your body type and decide what you want to accent and what you want to detract from. For example, bra-tops are best for those who are big on top, while leggy girls might want to hide their middle with a tankini. Take time to get the right size – too small and too big are equally disastrous.

250 AND THE PANEL SAYS ...

If you're worried about your width, go for a swimming costume that is shaded dark down the sides with a pale panel in the middle. This will help slim and flatter your figure.

251 HOW TO WEAR A STRING

If you are choosing a string bikini, make sure you know how to tie it. The bottom tie should rest on the hipbone, with the remaining string across your hip no longer than 18 cm (7 in). To tie the top, make a bow at the back first and then stretch the cups over your breasts to tie the neck. There should be no more than 5–8 cm (2–3 in) of string between your breasts.

252 CHOOSING A ONE-PIECE

When selecting a one-piece, make sure it is long enough to stay in place when you walk, otherwise it will ride up. Stand, sit, bend and walk in it before you buy to ensure that the suit is comfortable is snug enough to cup your bottom without cutting in. If it bulges or cuts, try a bigger size; if it droops, try a smaller one.

253 BELLY FLOP

If you don't like your tummy, try a tankini or look for an all-in-one that has a lower back to draw attention to a more flattering area.

254 TRY IT ON

When shopping for swimwear, try on as
many different styles as you can, as those
you might have dismissed in the past –
such as strings, halter-necks or boy short
styles – may actually suit your figure. Even
a 1940s high-waisted style might give
you an old-school glamour that suits
your personality.

255 CHOOSE A ONE-PIECE

Every wardrobe should contain at least one
one-piece swimsuit, whether you swim
for sport or not, for moments when you
want more coverage. The most fashionable
ones have unique shapes such as triangle
tops, plunging v-necks or cutaway areas, or
incorporate details such as rings or belts.

256 TRIED AND TRUE

If you are having difficulty finding a
swimsuit that fits well, bring along your
old favourite when you next go shopping.
The salesperson may be able to find a
near-enough match with an up-to-date
pattern or styling.

257 SKIRT THE ISSUE

Perfect for giving a bit more coverage across the bottom but with a youthful appeal, bikinis with little skirts are cute and trendy. Look for one that's slightly longer than the boy short. Like the ra-ra skirt, they do look best on those with narrow hips as they cut across the wide part of the hips.

258 HAVE AT LEAST FOUR

Make sure you have a collection of swimsuits for all situations and for numerous changes, especially if you take more than one beach holiday a year. Have at least four: two that provide more coverage and can be worn for swimming lengths and two for tanning.

259 BEWARE OF WHITE

White swimsuits look stunning with a tan and suit most colourings, from brunettes to blondes, but the last thing you want is transparency. Make sure it has double or triple lining, and put your hand inside the suit to see if you can see it through the fabric – if you can when it's dry, it will be very sheer when wet.

organizing your wardrobe

260 HAVE A CLEAR-OUT

Streamline your unruly clothes collection into a flexible, stylish wardrobe that works for you by having a giant clear-out. Throw everything onto the bed and take a long, critical look at what's there. Be ruthless when throwing things out – every item has to earn its keep.

261 APPLY THE TWO-YEAR RULE

Stick to the 'two-year rule' – if it hasn't been worn in that time, you won't miss it and it's time it went!

262 MIND THE GAP

Watch out for gaps in your wardrobe. For example, you might have plenty of great tops, but a serious shortage of skirts and trousers to wear them with. Shop cleverly to make all the clothes in your wardrobe work hard.

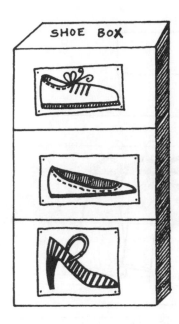

264 STORING SHOES

Shoe racks, boxes or shoe wardrobes are all options for organizing your shoes, and it does depend on the space you have available. Transparent plastic shoe containers are an excellent choice as you can easily see the shoes from the outside, and they have slide-out compartments so you won't be stacking or unstacking boxes.

265 PUT CLOTHES IN ORDER OF COLOUR

Arrange your clothes by colour – for example, red, orange, yellow, green, blue, and so on, interspersing white and black between the brightest shades. It makes your wardrobe look pretty and gives you fresh ideas on what clothes to mix and match.

263 SNAPPY SHOES

Store shoes in their boxes to keep them protected, but write their colour, shape and size on the top so you know what's in each box without having to open everything up. Or be super-organized and take a Polaroid of each pair and stick this on the front of the box.

266 ONLY KEEP WHAT FLATTERS

Hold on to what suits you. Don't keep 15 pairs of OK-fitting trousers – throw out all but the most flattering. Make sure you have different lengths of trousers to wear with heels and with flats, plus if you have short legs, have any over-long trousers taken up so they look as if they were made just for you.

267 LIKE WITH LIKE

For a neat, streamlined effect, hang similar items of clothing together – long dresses, suits, shirts, trousers and so on. This ensures you can always find what you're looking for in a flash.

268 SPACE-SAVER

For extra storage space, buy cardboard boxes and drawers to utilize the dead space at the bottom of your wardrobe. They're great for keeping belts, scarves and bags in order and can be found in pretty colours and prints.

269 THE GREAT DIVIDE

Plastic drawer dividers are a great buy and will really help you get organized. Use them for separating your knickers, socks and tights for fast access in the mornings. Divide into whites, colours and blacks. It's also worth separating black, navy and brown tights so you don't pick the wrong colour on a dark morning.

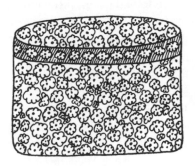
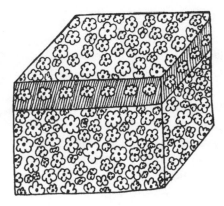

270 WINTER STORAGE

Put freshly laundered winter sweaters in paper bags (not plastic) for storage during the summer months. T-shirts, scarves and jeans can all be stored in this way in the winter, too.

271 GET RID OF GREYS

Every three months, have an underwear clear-out. Throw out anything that is greying – and replace it. Discard tights as soon as they ladder (run); don't put them away thinking they'll do for under trousers or you'll end up with a drawer full of hosiery that you can't wear with skirts.

272 PACK THEM IN

Never hang up silk or woollen sweaters. Always fold and place them on shelves using layers of tissue paper where possible.

273 MAKE A DONATION

Give away any 'mistakes' you've bought. Even if they're expensive and you feel guilty for not wearing them, it's pointless hanging on to clothes if they're just taking up valuable wardrobe space.

274 CHALK IT UP

Keep your nicely decluttered wardrobe damp-free by hanging up chalk tied on a length of string. The chalk sticks help to reduce moisture in the air and keep your wardrobe smelling fresher.

275 GO WIRELESS

Buy some good-quality wooden or padded hangers and throw away freebie wire ones that can damage the shape of your clothes.

276 GROUP AND ROTATE

Group together all your trousers, skirts, dresses and jackets so you know exactly where to find things. If something moves to the back, bring it to the front. You will find this means you wear all your clothes an equal amount instead of always choosing the same old thing.

277 THROW AWAY TAT

Anything with irreparable holes or splits should be thrown away, no matter how much you like it. You'll never feel good in clothes that have seen better days.

278 STORE IT WELL

Keep evening and wedding dresses in large, nylon garment bags designed for the job. Alternatively, store them in boxes with acid-free tissue (which insects do not like) to keep them in good condition.

279 SUCK IT IN

Vacuum packing is a cheap and safe way to store clothes, and it's also space-saving. Buy special bags fitted with a round rubber hole that allows an ordinary vacuum cleaner nozzle to be inserted to suck out all the air.

280 WARDROBE MATTERS

Forget trendy clothes rails. Your clothes need to be kept away from sunlight and dust in a wardrobe with doors if you want them to last.

281 JADED JEWELLERY

Is your jewellery box full of knotty chains you can't undo and broken bits of beads and pieces you can't wear? Either throw them out or take them to a jeweller's to be repaired.

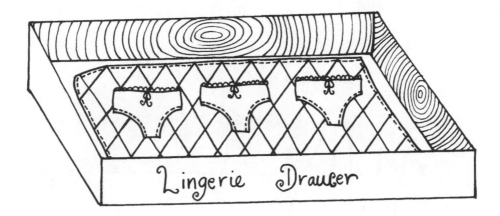

Lingerie Drawer

282 LINE YOUR DRAWERS

Protect your clothing from wood acid, which can cause fabric to deteriorate, by lining your clothes drawers with acid-free paper or quilted fabric. Never use wallpaper remnants – the sweet-smelling backing can attract insects to your clothing.

283 BEAT THE MOTHS

Moths love nothing more than cashmere and silk, so avoid giving them an expensive meal by ensuring your clothes are clean when you put them away (sweat and food stains attract moths) and invest in some cedarwood mothballs.

284 FLOWER POWER

Not only do sachets of lavender placed in drawers and hung in wardrobes leave your clothes smelling sweet, but they also deter insects, which hate the scent.

286 NEAT AND TIDY

Fold up all your sweaters and chunky-knit cardigans then pile them up on shelves according to colour and weight. This helps keep their shape for longer and allows you to see what you have at a glance. Place darker tones at the bottom and move through to lighter colours on top.

285 NO PLASTIC

Don't leave garments in plastic boxes or bags for more than three months. Sudden changes in temperature from central heating going on and off cause condensation in the container that dries on the garments and can cause mildew or yellowing on light colours. Rattan trunks instead are perfect for storing clothing as they allow it to breathe when air circulates through.

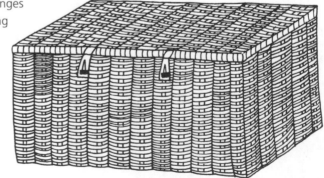

looking slimmer

287 THE RIGHT SIZE

There's no point in getting a size smaller simply because you hate having to buy the size you really are. In fact, a smaller size will be tighter and actually make you look bigger. If it really bothers you, cut the labels out (most are inaccurate anyway!) but buy clothes that fit and flatter.

288 FLAUNT IT!

Instead of concentrating on the parts of your body that you want to hide, focus and flaunt your positive points – sexy ankles, pretty toes, great lips, silky shoulders – everyone has something.

289 LONG AND LEAN

Wide-legged and bootcut trousers are great for any shape of body. While many think wide-legged trousers make legs look heavier, they create a straight line from the hips to the floor that creates a longer and leaner silhouette.

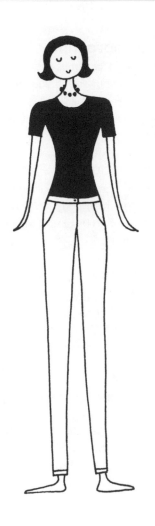

290 WALK TALL

Stand with your shoulders back, your back straight and your head held high. This simple trick will elongate your body and make you appear at least a size thinner.

291 CHOOSE CLOTH CAREFULLY

Avoid stiff and heavy fabrics or anything too clingy such as thin jersey or Lycra that will show off all the bits you want to hide. Opt instead for lightweight fabrics such as cashmere or fine-weave cotton that skim your curves rather than stick to them.

292 GRACEFULLY GREY

While it's true that wearing dark colours makes you look slimmer, you don't always have to restrict yourself to black. Navy, charcoal or dark grey all have the same flattering effect and are less harsh on paler skin tones.

293 MAKE PATTERNS WORK FOR YOU

Small patterns can make larger shapes look smaller, while the smaller you are, the larger the pattern you can carry off.

294 DOWN, NOT ACROSS

Horizontal lines can make you look wider, while verticals and pinstripes are much more flattering and make you seem much taller.

295 GET IT IN PROPORTION

Choose your accessories with care according to your size. If you are a larger woman, wearing small, delicate pieces of jewellery will actually make you appear bigger than you really are.

296 HORSING AROUND

It may sound simple but pulling your hair up into a high ponytail gives the appearance of an instantly thinner face and a longer neck.

297 FASHION BLOCK

Wearing the same colour all over will slim you, but this can look a bit dull every day. Try wearing the same tones rather than block colour all the way down.

298 DARK HORSE

Although scientists aren't sure why this is, it's a fact that a tan gives the illusion of a slimmer figure. But stick to fake tans rather than baking in the sun or using sunbeds – both of which can cause premature ageing and skin cancer.

300 NO NIPS AND TUCKS

Avoid darts and pleats as they will prevent clothes from sitting properly on your body and make you appear as if you are carrying extra weight.

301 GO RETRO

Body-slimming garments such as control pants and corsets might seem old-fashioned but they're perfect when you need an instantly sleeker, more structured body shape under dresses or skirts.

302 HIPS FOR BELTS

Avoid wearing belts around your waist if your problem area is your tummy. Loose hipster styles are ideal to detract the eye from pot-bellies.

299 V FOR VERY SLIM

Choose a top with a deeper v-neck than you normally wear as this will make your waist seem thinner. It's an optical illusion because it makes your shoulders look broader, going to a thin point just above your waist.

303 SKIRT AROUND IT

If you're not confident about your legs, choose the length of your skirt carefully. Skirts that fall just above the knee can make legs look stumpy. Mid-thigh or just-below-the-knee lengths are much better bets as they emphasize slim calves.

304 BALANCING ACT

If you are bottom-heavy and small on top, choose bright or patterned tops or ones with flattering necklines that draw the eye upwards. But if you're the other way round, do the reverse and go for detailed trousers or skirts.

305 CUT-OFF POINT

The longer the length of your trousers, the thinner they will make your legs look. Teaming long trousers with a pair of heels doubles the result. Cut-offs, pedal-pushers and shorts, on the other hand, all steal length from your legs.

306 JACKETS OFF

When wearing a jacket, make sure you're happy to take it off. If your jacket is covering a multitude of sins, such as a top that makes you look (or feel) fat or jeans that create bottom bulge, you'll feel compelled to keep it on. Wear a slimming, fitted cotton top underneath and carry a scarf to drape over yourself if it makes you feel more confident when you take your jacket off.

307 NO BUTTS

A hipster waistband or a top pulled down to hip-bone length over a pair of trousers instantly reduces the size of your butt.

308 WORK THOSE HEELS

High heels elongate your body, but avoid ankle straps as they cut off the legs, making them look shorter. Spindly heels are also a no-no as they can emphasize bigger calves. To make legs look longer and daintier, go for thicker heels and a pointed toe.

309 A-STUDENT

Wearing a dark-coloured A-line skirt that flows from the waist teamed with a fitted top draws attention upwards and makes a large bottom half appear smaller.

310 IT'S IN THE WRISTS

Three-quarter-length sleeves hide flabby upper arms while showing off the more flattering wrist section. Emphasize slim wrists with pretty delicate jewellery or chunky wooden bangles.

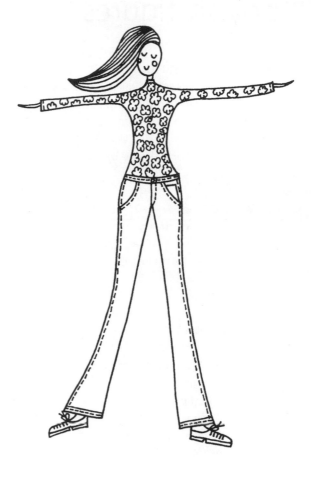

boyish figures

311 YOU'VE A BOYISH FIGURE IF ...

Your bust and hips are a similar width, your bust is fairly small and you have no defined waist. Your bottom is probably neat and flat and you have long slim legs. Make the most of your body shape by using the following tips ...

312 IT'S A CINCH

Athletic or boyish-shaped women lack a defined waist but you can create one with a wide eye-catching belt. Cinch it over a loose blouse and full skirt for maximum effect.

313 BE A SHADY LADY

Use shading to emphasize certain body parts. For example, use lighter colour where you want to fill out (across the bust) and a darker shade when you want to go in (at the waist), then lighter colour again at the hips. This creates a more hourglass illusion.

314 ONWARDS AND UPWARDS

Find ornate necklaces and earrings to draw attention to your slender neck and shoulders. Picking strong, bold jewellery will draw the eye upwards to one of your best features.

315 DEAD CERT

Shirts can look too masculine on boyish figures but a cleverly cut white shirt with a small ruffle at the neck and a waist tie will soften your look and add a waist while still being smart enough for work.

316 SHOW SOME LEG

Because you have naturally long legs, you are lucky enough to suit most hemline lengths, so make the most of your legs by wearing a mini. Make it an A-line shape, not tight, so the skirt gives you more of a waist.

317 PERFECTLY WRAPPED

Look out for wrap dresses in clingy soft jersey that have weight and hang well. The diagonal line of the dress creates the illusion of shape. Add a belt for extra definition to give you a waist and curvier hips.

318 BULK OUT

Belted coats with pockets on the hips add bulk and emphasize your hips and waist. A mac with padded shoulders also provides width on top, making your waist seem narrower. Make sure the belt is a different colour to add the impression of extra curves.

319 GO WITH THE FLOW

Choose soft and flowing, floaty fabrics that skim and soften your shape to add femininity. Bootcut jeans with a soft, girly chiffon blouse look sexy on slim boyish figures.

320 PLENTY OF PUFF

A floaty shirt with puff sleeves helps to soften broad shoulders and flatters skinny upper arms. Choose a round neck to emphasize a delicate collarbone and draw attention away from a small bust.

321 FAKE IT

For a special occasion or a night out, fake your shape. Use structured clothing such as a sexy basque or a laced corset top with hipster jeans.

322 EASY, TIGER!

While most women are advised to steer clear of horizontal stripes, boyish figures can easily get away with them because of your slim upper-body shape. They will also help to create the illusion of a bigger bust.

323 FLOWER POWER

Tulip- or bell-shaped skirts are clever and sexy choices for those with a boyish body shape as they create instant curves at the hips.

324 PRINTED STATEMENT

Your slim upper body means you can get away with gorgeous prints – which look fussy on bigger-busted types. These will give you an extra touch of femininity and again help to create the impression that your bust is bigger than it is.

325 SEXY SLEEVES

A good choice of top for your shape is a sleeveless style with a ruffled or detailed panel running down the front. The frills will hide a small chest while the sleeveless cut shows off slim, toned shoulders and arms.

326 THE FULL MONTY

Wear full or pleated skirts to help create the
illusion of a fuller figure. Add a fitted, shaped
top to avoid a bloated look. Pleated tops
are feminine and draw the eye away from a
straight body shape, but they can be too
much with a full skirt.

327 DON'T GET IN A FLAP

Avoid flapper-style 1920s dresses with
dropped waists. They will make you look
even more boyish and flat-chested and will
hide what little definition you have. Choose
fitted, waisted styles that push your bust up
and make your hips swing.

328 DON'T GO TOO LOW

If you're small on top, avoid highlighting this by
wearing low-cut tops. Round or slash necks are
good, or a small v-neck can also be flattering.

329 NOT SO HIGH

High-waisted trousers are not the most
flattering choice for women of this body
shape as they will eliminate curves and make
you look even longer than you are.

330 TROUSER TRICKS

If your legs are long and thin, then skinny jeans and straight satin cigarette trousers can look great on you. Make sure you wear a different shape on top, such as a loose-fitting cotton top cinched in at the waist or an empire-line blouse, to avoid the 'beanpole' look.

331 RIDE IT OUT

Fitted riding-style jackets will look great on your slim frame. Go for styles with added Lycra in the fabric, so that when you do up the top button they highlight your waist without looking too pulled-in.

332 DON'T BE SQUARE

Steer clear of boxy cropped jackets, shrugs and boleros – your lack of waist will be on full display. Make sure any jacket, cardigan or coat nips in at the waist.

333 DITCH THE DYNASTY LOOK

Avoid anything with padded shoulders – it will give you a rectangle shape and draw attention to your lack of curves.

334 GIVE SUITS THE BOOT

Unless they're well cut with lots of Lycra in the fabric, avoid very tailored trousersuits, which can make you look mannish and shapeless. Jackets should be fitted at the waist to create shape.

335 WIDE OF THE MARK

Steer clear of wide-legged trousers – they can make your bottom look invisible and hide any shape that you do have. Fitted slim or bootcut are best.

hourglass figures

336 YOU'VE AN HOURGLASS FIGURE IF ...

Your waist is narrow but your hips and shoulders are wide. You have a good-sized bust and tend to carry fat equally over your whole body. Your stomach is flat and toned but your thighs have a tendency to look heavy. Use the following tips to maximize your shape ...

337 TEA FOR TWO

Forties-style tea dresses are made for your figure. Similar to today's shirtdresses, they're wider on the bust and narrow at the waist, curving over the hips and narrowing again at the legs to make the most of your womanly shape.

338 FAB FORTIES AND FIFTIES

The styles of the 1940s and 1950s are perfect for you. Choose belted jackets and pencil skirts. Opt for tailored styles and stretch fabrics to sculpt and tame your curves. Remember to wear heels to balance heavy thighs and make calves look slim.

339 THIGH DISGUISE

Hide thicker-than-you'd-like thighs under full skirts. Wear with a shirt tied at the waist and a heel to make you look more slender.

340 THE THIN END ...

Choose thinner belts over wide or you'll look like the proverbial egg timer. Thinner belts flatter without being over-the-top for your figure.

341 MAKE A CROSSOVER

Dresses or tops that cross over at the waist look good and emphasize a great cleavage. Balance a top with wide-leg trousers and make sure the skirt of the dress is full enough to balance out your shape and prevent you looking top-heavy.

342 WHAT LIES BENEATH

Invest in good-quality underwear to give your bust and bottom great support. Try sexy seamless shorts and full-figure bras to avoid seams and lines showing through your clothes.

343 PENCIL POWER

High-waisted pencil skirts accentuate curves and a toned waist. They look dressed up enough for the office and will take you effortlessly into the evening.

344 WALK TALL

Medium-height heels should be the hourglass woman's best friend – they help you avoid looking too dumpy and elongate and thin the legs.

345 GOT IT? FLAUNT IT

Don't try to hide your body under baggy tops and loose trousers – you'll just look bigger than you are. Make the most of your shape by wearing well-fitting tops and tailored bottoms for everyday elegance.

346 BOXING CLEVER

Structured cropped jackets and boxy shapes that end on the bottom of the hip add proportion to your top half and draw attention to your narrow waist.

347 STICK THE BOOT IN

When it comes to choosing the most flattering trouser shape for you, bootcut wins every time as it helps to balance out wider hips. Go for dark denim jeans and black trousers – they will also make your thighs look thinner.

348 HIDE AND PEEP

Round-toed shoes and peep-toed heels are the best shape of shoe for you: they match the curves of your body and give you a 1950s sex-kitten look.

349 WORK THE SLEEVES

Three-quarter-length sleeves flatter larger arms and balance out a curvy bust and torso. Sleek and slim sleeves that taper at the elbow are flattering and bat-wing sleeves hide heavy upper arms.

350 GET IT IN THE NECK

V-necks flatter large busts and a generous cleavage, but don't spoil the effect by cluttering the neckline with chunky jewellery. Avoid square-necks – they can make you look wide and top-heavy.

351 GET INTO PRINT

There's no need for hourglass figures to avoid prints, but make sure they're not too overpowering. It's best to restrict them to your bottom half with a plain-coloured T-shirt or sweater on top.

352 THE LONG AND THE SHORT OF IT …

Very short skirts are not a great idea if you have wide hips and heavy thighs. But if you can't resist, try woollen tights in the same shade as the skirt for a slimming effect.

353 DIRE STRAIGHTS

Although untailored clothes are unflattering on your figure, so too are styles that are cut too straight. You need some extra room to allow for curves, so look for fabric that has some stretch or a garment with darts.

354 DON'T BE A BAG LADY

Baggy, untailored clothes just hide your curves and make you look heavier than you are. Make sure all your clothes have some structure.

355 THE SKINNY ON JEANS

While skinny jeans may be in fashion they do nothing to flatter your shapely figure. The tapered ankle and snug fit will make your hips and thighs look bigger than they are. Wide-leg or bootcut styles work best for you.

356 STICK YOUR NECK OUT

Polo necks will make you look even bigger than you are if you have a large bust. Instead, show your neck to elongate your décolletage and body.

357 BUTTON IT

Go for shirts where the buttons stop just above the bust to boost your cleavage instead of making it looked trapped! Fitted shirts that go in at the waist will flatter your figure.

358 CHUNKY MONKEY

Although they may be warm, thick knits can make you look extra bulky, so instead go for thin lamb's wool and cashmere sweaters. Team them with pretty scarves to add detail.

359 GET SHORTY

As with short skirts, city shorts can also be difficult for hourglass women to carry off. Don't go for skimpy hotpant-style shorts – they will only make your thighs and hips look bigger. If you are keen to wear them, pick a longer length in dark colours that you can team with dark tights and heels.

360 STAY IN SHAPE

Layering is difficult for your shape because you can quickly look bulkier. Choose thin fabrics and if you are wearing a few layers, add a belt so you don't lose your shape.

361 KEEP IT SIMPLE

Avoid too much fussy detail – ruffles, bows, ties and so on – as they will only overwhelm your shape. Stick to garments that are simple, elegant and streamlined.

pear shapes

362 YOU'VE A PEAR SHAPE IF ....

You are small-breasted and have a small waist with curvy, wider hips, a rounded bottom and heavy thighs. You may also have a slender neck and sloping shoulders. Try the following tips to flatter your bottom-heavy shape ...

363 MIND THE GAP

Hipster trousers are good for getting rid of the gaping waist problem often suffered by small-waisted pear-shapers. Look for low trousers or jeans that sit neatly on the hips and draw attention to a tiny waist.

364 BELOW THE WAIST

Trousers and skirts with waistlines that sit slightly below the natural waistline flatter pear-shaped hips. Without extra layers close to the smallest part of your waist, you can make it look smaller and your torso seem a little longer.

365 HELLO SAILOR

Wide necklines such as boatnecks or scoop-necks can help 'stretch out' your narrow shoulders and balance out your bottom half.

366 SHOW OFF YOUR WAIST

Draw attention to your upper body and waist by wearing neat fitted tops with pretty necklines, patterns and colours. Baggy tops will cover your waist instead of highlighting it.

367 FLAT AT THE FRONT

Wear softly-pleated or flat-fronted trousers or skirts to emphasize your well-defined waist area and draw attention to your middle but away from your hips.

368 A-GRADE

Skirts with a slight A-line cut will skim over problem areas and smooth hips and thighs away. Stay away from tight pencil skirts and cigarette trousers at all costs, however. They will give you a strange square shape down below and play up all the parts you want to hide.

369 COLOURING IN

Avoid light-coloured bottoms – they will make you look even bigger down below and lightweight fabrics can highlight bumps. Stick to darker blues and browns that absorb the light, and wear paler shades on top.

370 DON'T POCKET IT

Pockets on the hips of trousers and skirts bulk you out and make you seem wider. Instead go for smooth lines and front- or back-fastening bottoms.

371 CROP FLOPS

Avoid cropped trousers as they can 'cut your legs off' and make them look shorter and your hips and thighs wider.

372 SKIRT AROUND IT

A-line skirts are by far the most flattering style for pear shapes as they slim the hips and emphasize your smaller waist area. Short, tight skirts should be avoided, however, as these will accentuate the tops of your thighs and divert attention to that problematic area below the waist.

373 ALL WRAPPED UP

Wear coats and jackets done up and with a belt around the waist where possible to give your shape definition and to make the most of your tiny waist and neat top half.

374 HIGH FASHION

Choose pretty jewellery and colourful scarves to draw the eye upwards, away from the hips and thighs.

375 DRESS IT UP

Wear a simple cotton dress over straight-legged jeans. The dress will flatter your top half and draw attention upwards, while the skirt covers your problem area and is balanced out by the jeans underneath.

376 DON'T GO FOR STRETCH

Avoid wearing skirts or trousers with elasticated waists. While they may solve the initial problem of a gaping waist, elasticated waists are really unflattering and will make you look wider. Opt for structured clothes with waists that sit more on the hips.

377 LUSCIOUS LEGS

If you're wearing boots and you also have heavy thighs, the more fitted and shapely the boots are, the better. They will help to balance you out and make your legs look thinner.

378 ON THE LINE

Don't wear skirts that are cut on the bias as they will cling to all your lumps and bumps, highlighting tums and bottoms. Skirts with straight lines are the most flattering styles for pear-shaped women.

379 SHRUG IF YOU DON'T KNOW

Draw attention to your upper half by wearing sequined or brightly coloured shrugs or tiny cardigans. Styles that tie under the bust are especially flattering for those with a smaller top half.

380 BALANCE IT OUT

Pear-shaped women characteristically have slimmer shoulders than hips, so even out your shape by picking tops and shirts with puffed sleeves.

381 KNEES UP

Go for dresses and skirts that end just above the knee and in the winter team them with dark-coloured straight boots to hide chunky calves.

382 WIDE-LEG SAILOR STYLES

Though it may seem that wide legs could make you look larger than you are, you will actually look long and lean in sailor-style wide-legged trousers. They are great for pear shapes as they create a straight line from the hips to the hem.

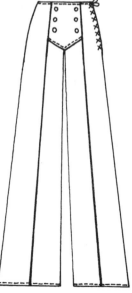

383 IN THE DARK

Dark-coloured trousers with a wide leg suit your shape best as they skim over your heavier bottom and thighs.

384 MIX IT UP

Mix up the layers and lengths you wear on your upper half. This will help to make your top and bottom halves appear more equal – and your bust will seem bigger, too.

385 BE A FIFTIES HOUSEWIFE!

Follow the 1950s trend and go for skirts and dresses that have a full skirt to hide your heavier bottom half.

apple shapes

386 YOU'VE AN APPLE SHAPE IF YOU ...

You have full breasts and a wide back, slim arms and wide shoulders, slim hips and legs plus a small, rounded bottom with a soft, rounded tummy. Make the most of your body shape by using the following tips ...

387 HANG LOOSE

Try loose, unstructured jackets over slim-fitting dresses to even out your figure.

388 LOSE THE MUFFIN

Wear shirts that extend lower than your waist to reduce the chances of any 'muffin top' – that is, a roll of flesh escaping between where your shirt meets your trousers. If you like your hips to look a little more in balance with your bust, try a shirt that meets the largest point of the hips.

389 SNAKE HIPS

Accentuate the narrowness of your hips with sexy and straight-fitting skirts. Wear a low-fitting belt at an angle to detract from any lack of waist. Shorter-length skirts will also show off your great legs but keep flow from your top to your bottom half so your mid section isn't emphasized.

390 DON'T BE CLINGY

Choosing the right material for your shape is very important. Don't go for tops created from tight-fitting material such as Lycra, as they will cling to every lump and bump. Tailored clothes made of cotton will always be more flattering on your shape.

391 SLIMMING TRICKS

Don't wear thin belts done up tightly across your tummy. This only draws attention to your problem area. A wider belt worn loosely on the hips that lies in a v-shape or diagonally will elongate your top half and make you look thinner.

392 VERY JANE AUSTEN

The empire line that cinches in just below the bust is a good shape for apples. Try floaty empire-line tops to maximize your cleavage and draw attention away from your waist.

393 HANG LOOSE

Skirts that sit just below the waistline with a brightly coloured belt or band will draw attention away from your waist and highlight your slim hips.

394 MOVING ON UP

Choose a shirt with a slightly lower neckline to keep the eyes moving upwards. Pair it with a statement necklace for maximum effect.

395 CARDIGAN COOL

Three-quarter-length cardigans are great for hiding a multitude of sins for apples. Wear them with slim trousers and drape the belt (if they have one) loosely across your tummy for a nipped-in waist effect.

396 SLIMMER LINES

Choose a skirt with a full silhouette. A slightly top-heavy appearance will be reduced, and when paired with a slim-fitting long-line top, you'll look sleek and streamlined.

397 SKIM IT

Try a thin chiffon blouse over a cotton camisole to skim over a thicker midriff. Wear it open at the neck to highlight your bust.

398 BE BROAD-MINDED

Look for flowing, wide-legged palazzo trousers – these will create a more even look between your upper and lower halves and also flaunt your slim ankles.

399 HOT LEGS

Skinny trousers show off your fabulously slim legs and small bottom, but team them with a longer sweater or tunic to help slim your waist.

400 LOSE THE PINCH

Don't wear tight miniskirts – they will dig into your waist and make you seem heavier on top than you really are. Try looser A-line styles that sit on the hips and create the illusion of a small waist.

401 COLOUR ME SIMPLE

Avoid mixing and matching lots of different colours. Choose monochromatic outfits – the use of just one colour will create an overall impression of length that takes the focus away from your width.

402 GO TO GREAT LENGTHS

When buying a trouser suit opt for a longer length jacket rather than a standard length as they can finish at an unflattering angle and draw attention to your tummy.

403 TIGHT FIT

Keep away from very fitted or tailored suits, particularly those with well-defined waistbands, as they will only draw unwanted attention to your mid-section.

404 NO JACKET REQUIRED

Because of your big bust and top half, you should avoid double-breasted jackets as they make you seem bigger than you are.

405 POCKET IT

Pockets at the waist area should be avoided by apples – they can be unflattering and attract unwanted attention to the upper body.

406 THIN END OF THE WEDGE

Embrace chunkier-style shoes such as wedges. Wearing a slightly heavier shoe can help to anchor and balance your top half.

407 STICK TO SIDEWAYS

Look out for trousers that do up at the sides – this will keep your stomach area looking more streamlined.

408 PERFECT YOUR PINS

Wear short skirts with bare legs or flesh-coloured tights to draw attention to your shapely legs.

409 GET KNITTED

Thin knits tend to pull over apple-shaped tummies. Go for slightly heavier wools and cottons in bright colours to skim and flatter your mid-section.

410 FLATTEN THAT TUMMY

Shirts with a zip on the side flatten your middle because they're fitted and shaped.

411 COME UNDONE

If you're wearing a tailored jacket with a suit, keep the jacket undone so that it doesn't look as if you're fighting to keep your tummy in.

412 GIVE US AN 'A'

A-line skirts and dresses are a good choice for your shape as they give the body definition while hiding all your least favourite bits.

troubleshooting body flaws

414 FULLER BUST

A sleeveless turtleneck diverts attention away from a busty upper body by emphasizing the arms. Similarly, a cropped jacket draws the eye to the waist. Always wear a bra that fits you properly and has adequate support to lift your boobs.

415 HEAVY LEGS

Bootcut trousers and skirts with a small side split work well on larger legs. Wear trousers and skirts that are on the large side rather than too tight – anything that appears to be straining at the seams will make you look bigger.

413 MAKE LIKE A SWAN

When it comes to necklines, apple-shaped women often have quite short necks so lengthen yours with a low neckline and a long pendant necklace.

416 THICK WAIST

Men's-style shirts tucked into trousers and skirts with sexy heels camouflage the middle area and add Katharine Hepburn-style chic.

417 CANKLES

If you have calves that somehow don't seem to extend and taper down to ankles, resist the temptation to wear trousers all the time. You can still wear dresses and skirts. Create slimmer ankles by wearing skirts that stop at the knee and shoes with medium-height heels that aren't too thin.

418 BIG BOTTOM

A long-line blazer will hide your behind and give you the confidence to wear a body-fitting dress or a pair of straight-leg jeans. Avoid G-strings as they can accentuate a large backside. Choose hipster briefs instead, with plenty of Lycra support to lift your bum and prevent it looking saggy.

419 WIDE HIPS

Choose A-line skirts in plain colours to minimize wide hips. You should also avoid shiny, satin fabrics or bright-coloured skirts and trousers that will draw attention to saddlebags and create a wider silhouette.

420 THICK ANKLES

Don't wear strappy, delicate heels as will they draw attention to the area. Also avoid flat, ballet pump-type shoes or those with ankle straps, which cut across the ankle and make it look bigger.

421 LOSE THOSE LOVE HANDLES

Floaty tops and A-line skirts miraculously hide extra flesh around the hips and waist. Structured clothing such as well-tailored jackets will also help.

422 VERTICALLY CHALLENGED

Long wide-legged trousers lengthen legs – especially when worn with high boots. Vertical pinstripes and front creases are also flattering if you want to look taller.

423 STUBBY LEGS

Shorter skirts make all women look taller but they don't have to be minis: just-above-the-knee will work, too. Avoid longer skirts that make you look as if you are standing in a hole, however.

424 BROAD SHOULDERS

Soften wide shoulders with cardigans, shrugs and fitted blouses. Avoid jackets and structured suits that will only emphasize angles and make you look wider.

425 SHORT BOTTOM HALF

Empire-waist dresses will lengthen your lower half. Try above-the-knee lengths as well to keep the look modern.

426 BULKY TOP HALF

Fitted, slightly tapered jackets give the appearance of a slimmer waist, neat shoulders and slim arms.

427 SHORT BODY

Keep jackets short and sweet – longer jackets will only make you look shorter.

428 BINGO WINGS

Cover less-than-slender arms in draped bell sleeves and light floaty fabrics. Resist the urge to wear bulky sweaters – they just make your arms look bigger.

429 LARGE FEET

Make big feet appear smaller in dark-coloured boots and trousers that are wide at the ankle. Bootcut trousers give the illusion of smaller feet, especially if worn with high wedge or platform boots.

430 FLAT BUM

Invest in some shaper support knickers to lift and give your bottom shape. Hipster jeans create the illusion of a small rounded bottom and add shape where there isn't any.

431 LOOSEN UP LOVE HANDLES

Try a layered look: wear a loose, open cardigan or tunic over a slim tee and trousers to give you a trim mid-section. You may need to go up a size in trousers, too, but pick a slim-cut style so they aren't too big through the legs and hips.

432 WIDE BOTTOM

Straight wide-legged trousers even out a wide bottom, especially when teamed with a fitted top and jacket.

433 DOUBLE CHIN

Avoid eye-catching jewellery at the neck. Draw the eye down to the waist and away from the problem area, and emphasize a great pair of legs in tight jeans instead. A polo (turtle) neck can also work wonders.

434 SLOPING SHOULDERS

Structured, fitted jackets and good tailoring do wonders for correcting posture. Necklines that go straight across will also make the shoulder area seem straighter.

436 SMALL BUST

Invest in a good padded push-up bra and don't shy away from tight tops. High-necked tops and polo necks in light colours add weight to the bust area as do horizontal stripes.

437 TUMMY FLAB

Disguise that little roll of belly flab with long, crisp men's-style shirts cinched in with a belt. Avoid hipster trousers unless worn with a long top – trousers and skirts that sit just on the waist are better.

438 THICK WRISTS

Chunky bangles make thicker wrists look smaller and more delicate. Try ethnic bangles and wide silver bracelets.

439 KNOBBLY KNEES

Avoid the obvious such as miniskirts but don't shun skirts and dresses altogether. A patterned frock worn with black opaque tights can even out the shape of your knees.

435 SHORT NECK

The ultimate lengthening trick is to wear the 'Sabrina' neckline – named after Audrey Hepburn's character in the film of the same name. It's a wide, shallow, straight neckline, sometimes called a 'boatneck', and was created by Hubert de Givenchy, who designed many of Hepburn's clothes.

casual daywear

440 IT'S A WRAP

For an all-purpose, wear anywhere, anytime outfit, a wrap dress is a great investment. Pick one in jersey fabric that drapes gracefully and will flatter almost every figure. Try a small geometric print for a modern look or invest in a solid colour that will work for evening, too.

441 CASUAL, NOT SCRUFFY

Don't skimp on the quality of casual clothes. Cheap fabrics look cheap and will deteriorate very quickly. Stick to 100% cottons, wools and silks with a little added Lycra to keep the shape and allow the garment some 'give'.

442 THE LONG AND SHORT OF IT

Don't wear sweaters that are too long over jeans if you're short – they'll only make you look smaller. Instead, try a fitted lamb's wool cardigan over a camisole or a shaped v-neck or polo.

445 CONSIDER LOSING THE LEGGINGS

Leggings under skirts can make you seem as if you're going for a ballet audition. Unless you're young and slim, and wear them under clothes as you would tights, they're not a good look. On their own they can make the slimmest look enormous.

443 STEAL CONTINENTAL STYLE

Classic, fitted open-necked shirts with a knotted scarf at the neck worn with jeans and boots or flats will take you anywhere with effortless chic. Dress the look up with a blazer or down with a cashmere sweater.

444 EASE YOURSELF INTO CASUAL

If you still prefer to wear suits for work and find it hard to dress down, liven the tailoring up with unexpected high-impact jewellery and funky shoes.

446 ACCESSORIZE RIGHT

Don't wear sparkly jewellery or anything too big with casual clothes – it will look bling-heavy. Keep it small and understated so you don't look as if you've tried too hard.

447 HAVE A PLAN

Buy your casual clothes in the same way as you choose career clothes. Don't just buy random comfy tops and bottoms, pick cohesive pieces and build them around basic styles. A good approach is three colours for the best mix-and-match wardrobe – khaki, denim and cream, or black, khaki and white. You can then throw colourful tops and accessories into the mix.

448 PERFECT FIT

Just because it's casual, this doesn't mean that big and baggy is OK. Even if it's simply a tracksuit or cotton trousers and a T-shirt, you will feel and look better if everything fits properly. If you really love oversized sweaters, make sure you team them with a belt and keep the trousers skinny.

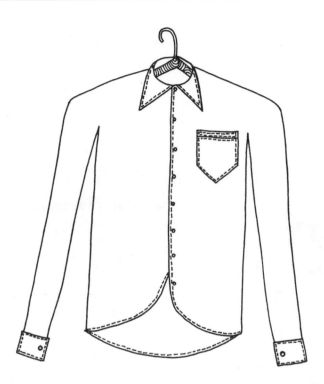

449 CASUAL CLOTHES CARE

Keep your casual clothes in good shape. You'll feel much better wearing clothes that are crisply ironed and clean even if it's just for the weekend.

450 DON'T LET YOUR SHIRT DO THE TALKING

No matter what anyone might say, T-shirts with slogans on them are distinctly tacky and best avoided unless you're a teenager.

451 GET THE COAT RIGHT

Don't ruin your look with a great big, shapeless coat. Invest in a short, shapely pea coat or a shaped parka. Sleeveless jackets look good with warm lamb's wool or cashmere sweaters. A cosy duffel coat in a pastel colour always looks pretty, too.

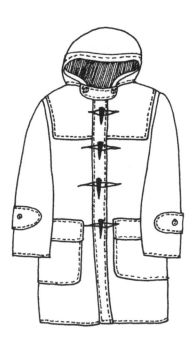

452 LAYERS ARE KEY

Effortless, relaxed dressing style is down to good layering. Camisoles under shirts or with a wrap cardie look great, as do long-sleeved T-shirts underneath short-sleeved tees in toning colours. A draped cardigan and well-cut jeans with a scarf will take you anywhere.

453 PERFECTLY POLISHED

It goes without saying that you should still be groomed if you're casual. Wrinkled, unironed or stained clothes with buttons missing, hems dropping or faded fabrics are a no-no wherever you are. Even relaxing at home you won't feel your best in tatty clothes.

454 LEAVE BEACHWEAR ON THE BEACH

Bikinis and swimsuits don't function as casual wear so save them for the sun-lounger. Bikini tops and sarongs look especially tacky in a city environment, no matter how hot it is and how much you want to show off your sexy, brown midriff. Save them for the beach.

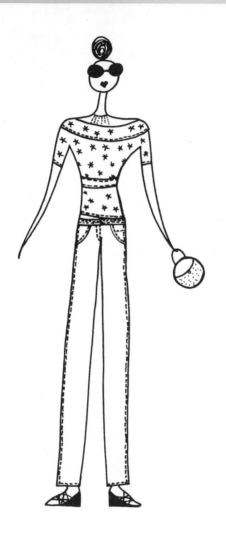

455 DRESS UP DENIM

Pair jeans with a sparkly top for an evening look that's relaxed and glamorous. The top says you've made an effort but the jeans say you haven't tried too hard. This is the one occasion when you should always wear a pair of heels.

456 FANCY FOOTWEAR

Find a great pair of casual shoes for the weekend – nothing kills a chic sporty look more than a pair of dirty white running shoes. Retro trainers such as Converse in colourful suedes, fur-trimmed boots and flat sandals are good choices with most casual wear.

457 DON'T BE TOO UPTIGHT

When you're wearing a tight shirt or top, wear loose trousers; with tight trousers, wear a loose shirt. Wearing loose with loose makes you look sloppy, while a tight top with tight trousers can look too body-conscious.

458 DRESSING DOWN

A shift dress can be casually chic in lots of different ways – worn over leggings, with tights as a minidress or with skinny jeans. A simple shirtdress in plain cotton or denim with boots or flat pumps is also surprisingly easy to wear. Go bare-legged in summer and wear with long boots in the winter.

459 IT'S IN THE DETAILS

A pair of designer shoes or an expensive bag can be a subtle way of telling the world that, for all your casual attire, you are someone to be taken seriously in the style stakes.

460 CASUAL CAN MEAN SUITS

Casual doesn't always have to mean jeans. Suits can be softly tailored to look good yet be easy to wear and comfortable with a fine knitted sweater or T-shirt underneath plus boots.

461 FLIP-ING COOL

Look on-trend in the summer by teaming cute floral dresses with flip-flops. Your feet will stay cool and you can carry off the casual shoe style if the rest of your outfit looks groomed.

smart-casual

462 NOT SHORT ON STYLE
Shorts have become incorporated into our smart-casual wardrobes, but it's all about picking the right length and cut. Slimline, knee-length city shorts are perfect for work, while anything above the knee should be kept for sports or holidays.

463 BE A YUMMY MUMMY
For school concerts and parents' evenings you can't beat a smart-casual look. You want to look sensible but not matronly so opt for chic linen trousers instead of jeans and knee-length skirts rather than minis.

464 ALWAYS DRESS FOR DINNER
The old adage that it's better to be over- than underdressed still holds true. No-one has ever been asked to leave a party because they looked too gorgeous!

465 GET A BEADED CLUTCH

Even for daytime, a stylish handbag adds panache to your special occasion ensemble. Invest in an all-purpose clutch decorated with subtle beading (avoid sequins and glitter, which are not so classic). But be sure it's big enough to hold a wallet, lipstick and keys.

466 DON A BLAZER

Need to smarten up a casual outfit in a hurry? Pulling on this wardrobe staple adds a touch of class to everything from simple white blouses to plain black trousers and jeans.

on the job

467 JUST THE JOB

First impressions are very important so make sure your future employer is not put off at first glance. You want to look smart and organized but not dull and dismal. Think chic trousers or skirt, an interesting shirt and a fitted long cardigan or jacket in similar, subtle colours.

468 BE SUIT-ABLY ATTIRED

A classic trouser suit is worth investing
a bit of money in – it should last a few
years. The better the quality of the fabric
and lining, the better the investment. A
good suit can be the most wearable outfit
you own as it can be dressed up or down,
the jacket can be worn separately with
jeans and the trousers or skirt with shirts.

469 SHOW YOUR PERSONALITY

While it's important to look together and
groomed you should also reveal a touch
of your personality to a potential employer
to ensure you stand out from all the rest.
Think about an unusual belt, brooch
or beaded necklace to add a touch of
individuality to your outfit.

470 TOSS THE TRAINERS

Don't wear trainers (sneakers) with jeans or
skirts. It's just too casual, even for the most
laid-back office, and won't make you look
or feel professional enough for work mode.
Smart pumps or boots are polished but not
over-done.

471 SLEEVES, PLEASE

Don't wear strapless tops to work, no matter
how hot it is. And even in a casual office,
avoid strappy spaghetti straps as they won't
look professional – you need to wear a bra
and the straps will always show. If you're
wearing something for going out that night,
keep a cute cardie on during the day.

472 IMPRESSING AT INTERVIEW

Do your research! Find out how formal the company is. However, even if the staff wear jeans from day to day, it's always better to attend an interview wearing something smarter.

473 GIVE SKIRTS A LIFT

For casual chic at the office, wear heels with skirts. Flats just don't look professional or polished and feel as if you're heading for a day at the beach, not an important marketing meeting. They don't have to be skyscrapers, just neat mid-heels to make the skirt look elegant.

office to evening

474 SHIMMER UNDER YOUR SUIT

Even the dullest office wear can be transformed into a look you can dance the night away in when paired with a glittery camisole or halterneck.

475 NIGHTS IN BLACK SATIN

Black straight-legged satin trousers worn with a cropped jacket and top look smart enough for the boardroom, and a quick change of top at the end of the day will leave you looking effortlessly cool for a party.

476 A SUITABLE STYLE

If you have to wear a suit to work, try choosing one that you can carry off easily from day to night. Go for a style that breaks from the norm or is in a colour other than black. A well-cut suit in a unique design can also be pieced separately, such as with a pair of smart jeans that you can then wear straight to the bar.

477 THE CLASSIC LBD

The little black dress is a versatile item that you can wear from office to evening. Wear to the office with flats and a chunky-knit cardigan and belt, then change into heels, add some jewellery and leave the cardigan in the cloakroom for an instantly glamorous evening look.

478 MAKE A STATEMENT

Adding some signature jewellery gives
sophistication to your day look. Think
bold earrings and pendants.

479 SEXY CLUTCHES

Don't let a huge workbag ruin your
evening look. Leave anything you don't
need in your drawer at work and take
out just the essentials in a smart and sexy
clutch bag.

party & formal

480 BAG THE STYLE AWARD

For work award events or balls you can
afford to go for full-blown glamour.
Long dresses or strapless 1950s styles
with full skirts will always make you look
extra-stylish. And go to town on your hair,
make-up and heels.

481 COCKTAIL HOUR

For black-tie and cocktail parties the look to go for is chic and poised. The hemline on the dress is not of such importance – but the width certainly is. Keep it streamlined and well cut instead of billowing and flouncy.

482 DRESS FOR BLACK TIE

A floor-length smart cocktail frock in a dark shade is great to have in your wardrobe as a fail-safe choice for black-tie events. Go for a classic cut to which you can add accessories and different pairs of shoes to bring it bang up-to-date each time you wear it.

483 HITTING THE RIGHT NOTE

Dressing up for the opera is not a necessity these days but it's a great excuse! If you are scared of being too over-the-top, choose a classic little black dress that you can team with heels and then make some extra effort with your hair, make–up and accessories.

484 GO TO MAXI LENGTHS

Many women are wary of long dresses but they are an easy way to get instant evening glamour, whether you're going to a ball or society event or attending the theatre or ballet. Team with simple accessories and an elegant clutch bag – and don't forget the heels!

485 BIRTHDAY BEAUTY

If it's your birthday you want to make sure you look your best. Plan in advance and treat yourself to something special. If you're going for a meal, remember you'll be sitting down most of the night, so make the most of a pretty top and statement jewellery.

486 CONCERT CHIC

Dressing for a concert should be about looking laidback with an edge. If you are heading off to a rock concert, skinny jeans, flat boots or pumps and a vintage T-shirt will give you an effortless rock-chick look.

487 NIGHTS IN COLOURED SATIN

For evening events, satin dresses can be a sexy alternative to more usual fabrics. Instead of keeping it safe in black, go for bright blue, pinks or purples.

at-home style

488 FUN WITH FRIENDS

If you're having friends over for a girly night, pretty cotton long-sleeved tops with loose comfy trousers are ideal. Wrap yourself in a brightly coloured pashmina to feel instantly cosy but glamorous.

489 GIRL NEXT DOOR

You can do sexy while lazing at home. Trying layering camisoles with soft comfy cardigans, long stretchy dresses or pull-ons – casual loose trousers – in lovely fabrics with toning T-shirts. Keep feet toasty with cashmere socks or warm Ugg boots.

490 PYJAMA PARTY

Stylish women get dressed even if they're not going out anywhere. The trick is to find clothes you would be happy to answer the door in. Try wide-legged palazzo trousers in luxury fabrics and matching T-shirts. Add a soft mohair ballerina-style cardie if it's chilly.

491 CHIC BUT COMFY

Casual jeans or a skirt with a glamorous top and shoes are great for entertaining at home, and can look artlessly elegant when accessorized with good jewellery.

492 CHECK IT FIRST

You will be getting up and down quite a lot if you're the host, so make sure you don't wear something that shifts around, exposes flesh, rides up or creases easily.

493 ACCESSORIZE WISELY

Wear a scarf around your head or to secure a ponytail to keep your hair out of the way, but avoid long sleeves or scarves that may prove to be a safety hazard in the kitchen!

date clothes

494 BE COMFORTABLE

Don't squeeze into something that doesn't fit or wear clothes that are not your style. You'll feel awkward and be concentrating on your outfit more than the flow of conversation.

495 PLAY DEMURE

Don't put everything out on display on a first date. It might grab his attention at the time – but possibly only because he thinks his luck's in! Retain a bit of mystery to keep him interested for longer and stick to the golden rule of showing off your legs or chest but never both at the same time.

496 BE YOURSELF

Try wearing something that reflects your personality, such as a favourite bracelet or a quirky handbag. Not only will you feel more comfortable but this will also help your date to know a bit more about you.

497 COLOUR CONSIDERATIONS

Black might be flattering but you don't want your date to think you've just come back from a funeral. Safe colours include light blue, which has a calming affect, and pink, which exudes femininity and nurturing. However, research shows that red is the easiest colour on the eye and invokes life and passion – the perfect ingredients for the perfect date.

498 CHOOSE SHOES CAREFULLY

Make sure your shoes match your outfit and are suitable for your date – but most importantly, make sure you feel comfortable in them. You want to be enjoying the romance and not focusing on your sore feet.

499 DON'T LOOK LIKE A TRY-HARD

Chances are your date is unlikely to know his Hermès from his H&M, so don't feel the need to look as if you've just stepped out of the pages of a fashion magazine (unless of course you always do). Men often find high fashion a little scary.

500 GET THE DETAILS RIGHT

Before your date, find out where you are going to be going and what time you will be meeting. There's no point in wearing your newest high heels for an afternoon stroll in the country, while jeans and a smart top may not be dressy enough if your date is taking you out to the hottest new restaurant in town.

501 GO EASY ON THE BLING

You might understand the irony of wearing lots of gold but your date will just think you are trying to rival Mr T.

502 DON'T EXPERIMENT!

Wear garments and accessories in shapes and colours that you know you already look good in. He's not to know just how old your most flattering top is.

503 SMALL STUFF COUNTS

Complement your look by checking the little details work. You don't want to ruin your outfit with a scruffy bag or chipped nails.

504 PHONE A FRIEND

Ask a trusted friend for advice on your date outfit. They will be able to give you their honest opinion and save you from any embarrassment.

505 DON'T DRESS DOWN

Dress up slightly more than you would to meet a friend for a date. Not only will this mean that you won't end up looking too casual but it will also show your date that you have made an effort and that you are interested in him.

506 EASE UP ON KILLER HEELS

If your date is on the diminutive side you don't want to intimidate him by towering over him in your stilettos. And even tall men like to feel they tower over you a bit – it brings out their protective side!

507 STYLISH SMALLS

While your date might not get to see it, wearing lingerie that matches and fits well will give you inner confidence and an extra touch of sexiness.

508 TRIED AND TESTED

You can never fail with the trusty LBD. Add your favourite jewellery, scarf or bag to tie in with the location of your date and to show off your individuality.

509 STAND UP STRAIGHT!

Whatever you're wearing you will always look better if you have great posture. Stand with your shoulders back and your head held high and you'll instantly look and feel thinner and more confident.

510 EASE THE PRESSURE

Never plan to buy an outfit on the day of the date. It is unlikely that they will have your size in the dress that you want and you'll end up feeling extra stressed with nothing to wear.

511 FLAUNT AND FLATTER

Flaunt your best asset and flatter your least. If you have endlessly long legs, show them off in a short skirt. You can worry about him seeing your wobbly bits at a later time.

512 DON'T GO IN DISGUISE

Dress for yourself first and your date after. If the first meeting goes well, you don't want to feel forced to wear clothes that are not really you every time you get together.

513 BE WARY OF WHITE

Although you may want to appear sweet and innocent by wearing lots of white clothing, it can also make you look pale and shows up yellow teeth. Plus you don't want to be worrying about dropping food or drink down it for the entire date.

514 KNOWLEDGE IS POWER

If you know your date likes a certain article of clothing on you, use it to your advantage and experiment with different ways to wear it or buy similar-styled items.

515 DON'T GET IN A SWEAT

Be wary of clothes that have the ability to make you get a bit hot under the collar. Sweat patches are never a good look. Go for layers and clothes made of natural fibres that will let your skin breathe.

516 DON'T OVER- OR UNDERDRESS TO IMPRESS

A high-maintenance look can be as scary as overt sexuality on a date – if in doubt, keep it casual, clean and covered up!

517 ACCENTUATE THE LESS OBVIOUS

The neck, shoulders and back are some of the parts of the body that men find most alluring in women. Try a strapless top or a dress with a low back for a hint of sexiness without showing off too much skin.

518 DON'T WEAR JEWELLERY FROM YOUR EX

It may be beautiful but a lovely piece of jewellery will inevitably be brought up in conversation – if not on the first date then definitely on the second. Rather than making your new beau feel like he needs to compete with the ex, leave him out of the picture until the time is right for both of you to discuss your pasts.

519 CHECK THE FORECAST

Organize an alternative outfit in the event of unreliable weather. You don't want to be left shivering in a light cotton sundress during a summer shower. Additionally, be careful with white articles of clothing if you have to travel in the rain as they can easily become transparent when wet.

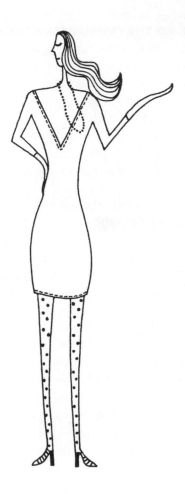

520 LEAVE THE FASHIONISTA AT HOME

Don't try to be too trendy. Leave experimenting with the most up-to-the-minute looks until later in the relationship.

521 IF ALL ELSE FAILS ...

Your favourite jeans with heels and a pretty top and blazer-style jacket is always a safe compromise that works for most situations.

522 LET YOUR PERSONALITY DO THE TALKING

Never let your clothes overpower what's beneath them. Wouldn't you rather your date remembered you for your great personality and sparkling eyes than because of your amazing Mulberry handbag?

523 DON'T COPY HIS LOOK

Just because your date dresses in a certain way doesn't mean that you should, too. You'll only end up looking a bit of a fake and as if you're trying too hard. Your date is there to find out about the real you, not to discover a female version of himself.

funerals & weddings

524 A SIGN OF RESPECT

Always ask about the dress code before going to a funeral. Sometimes people are asked to wear the deceased's favourite colour or not to wear black. If this is not the case, then black, navy or dark brown is the safest option. Go for smart, tailored knee-length skirts and fitted jackets. A soft, beige-coloured pashmina can break up the look. The main rule is to look smart and respectful.

525 NEVER UPSTAGE THE BRIDE

While you want to look your best at weddings, always remember that the bride should be the centre of attention, not you. Avoid wearing any real statement pieces or anything too flouncy and don't wear white unless it's the background colour to a pattern.

526 WARM AND WINTRY

Velvet is the ideal glamorous material to wear to a winter wedding or other events during the colder months. A velvet fitted jacket over a gold or silver top is the perfect item to keep you warm in a draughty church and this can then be discarded later on for the reception.

527 IN TUNE WITH THE SEASONS

As a general rule for a special event, try to match the colour of your clothes to the shade of the season. Darker berry colours mixed with blacks and greys work well in winter, while pastels and whites are great during the summer. For autumn, think browns, greens and oranges, and opt for pretty pinks and purples in springtime.

528 DARK NIGHTS, BRIGHT DAYS

Although black is very flattering, it is one colour that should be avoided at daytime weddings. It is more acceptable to wear black for the evening reception but try to cheer it up with jewellery and pretty shoes.

529 TOP HAT AND TAILS

If hats are required for a wedding, don't automatically make for the traditional wide-brim and big-bow wedding hat. Look for one with a certain style and individuality. For choice and a good fit, visit a department store or specialist milliner or hat designer.

530 FEATHER IN YOUR CAP

Instead of hats, look for large hair clips or statement headpieces made from feathers or bows for a more modern look. But remember, the fancier you go on top, the simpler your outfit below should be.

531 CHECK THE INVITE

Dress up more for weddings after 6 pm and keep things a bit more relaxed for morning and afternoon affairs. If the wedding is in the morning and the reception takes place in the evening, dress for the latter – the church service will be over more quickly than the reception and you don't want to feel uncomfortable all evening.

532 A TOUCH OF ELEGANCE

It's years since it was necessary for women to wear gloves to a wedding but that doesn't mean you can't. A delicate pair in white lace can give you an extra-stylish touch, while a smart leather pair will keep you warm in draughty churches and outside while all the photos take place.

533 BUY A FABULOUS COAT

If you are attending a winter wedding, don't ruin your amazing outfit with a dull coat. Go for frock coats in a block colour that tones with your outfit or pick one with a great pattern.

534 SAVE IT FOR THE BIG DAY

If you have been invited to an engagement party, you won't want to dress up as much as you would for the wedding, so keep your look fun and casual. A skirt with tights and heels or a summer dress with a cardigan and sparkly pumps means you will still look smart but can save the wow factor for the actual wedding.

535 CULTURAL CHIC

Invited to an event from another culture – a Hindu wedding, for example? Embrace the customs and fashions with the right jewellery, pretty scarves and dresses that extend below the knee – but don't copy traditional clothes exactly (unless invited to!) or you'll come across as having tried too hard.

536 QUICK COVER-UP

For a summer wedding, strappy dresses can look great but make sure you bring along a shawl or little cardigan to cover your shoulders in case the weather turns colder.

537 IT'S OK TO NOT MATCH

Don't worry about trying to fit into the wedding theme by wearing similar colours to the bridesmaids or mothers. There's no way you can co-ordinate with everyone attending the event. If the invitation doesn't offer advice, look at the style of the invitation itself – if it's formal, the wedding is likely to be too.

christenings

538 BABY BLUES

Christenings can be tricky to dress for. You want to look smart but not too 'wedding'. Think knee-length skirts and pretty sweaters or smart trousers with detailed shirts and tailored jackets.

539 SET A GOOD EXAMPLE

If you are going to be a godmother, it's even more important to get the right look. Cool, elegant and covered are the main rules. Don't even think about low-cut (no matter how attractive the priest!). You can't go wrong with classic navy, camel or ecru with small, chic accessories.

540 WEAR THE RIGHT HEEL

Remember that at a christening you may be expected to hold the baby at some point, so wear shoes that you can stand safely in and which won't cause you to topple over!

outdoor events

541 DON'T GET TOO BLOWN AWAY

Don't forget that racing horses can cause a fair amount of breeze when they speed past you – so make sure your hat is well secured and that your clothes aren't made of too flimsy material.

542 MUMMY COOL

Your child's sports day calls for loose trousers and a pretty summery top teamed with a soft, shaped cardie. And remember to wear flat ballet shoes or pretty flip-flops that you can discard effortlessly when you want to join in the parent's race!

543 DRESS TO THE MAX

For summer evening events where you'll be eating al fresco, stand out in style with a floor-length maxi dress. Choose from fitted to floaty, and spaghetti-straps to thicker halter-neck ties, and team with a cute cardigan.

544 DON'T GO OVERBOARD

For boat parties, avoid wearing anything too nautical themed as you could end up looking as if you've come in fancy dress! Smart wide-leg, dark trousers and three-quarter-length sleeve tops will keep you looking sophisticated yet warm, and save your modesty from sea breezes. Stick to flatties and keep your heels for dry land.

545 ROUGH AND TUMBLE

Jeans are perfect for outdoor parties. They're sexy, practical for dancing or games, they don't show grass or food stains easily and smart designer jeans are accepted pretty much anywhere. Team them with a glamorous summery top so you still look like you've made an effort.

546 BE WARY OF WHITE

For picnics and barbecues it's safest to avoid white. While it's normally a great summer choice, there's nothing worse than a red wine or ketchup stain putting a dampener on your day.

547 FESTIVAL FEET

Keeping your feet dry at rainy summer festivals is essential but this doesn't mean old and ugly brown wellies. Check out shoe shops for wellingtons in funky colours and patterns or go for a sturdy pair of cowboy boots instead.

548 PRACTICAL CHOICE

T-dresses may not seem the obvious choice for festivals but they are very versatile. Wear them over jeans for one look and with cowboy boots for another. Go for those with sleeves to protect your shoulders from burning in the sunshine. And don't forget a stylish raincoat for any wet days.

549 OUTDOOR ENTERTAINMENT

When attending an outdoor concert or play, think comfort and layers. If it takes place on a warm summer's afternoon, leading into a chillier evening, try dark linen trousers or wide knee-length skirts (so you can sit on the ground comfortably) with a camisole, cotton top and wrap cardigan.

550 SUMMER BREEZE

For outdoor summer events such as concerts or garden parties, you can't go wrong with a pashmina. Wear it across your shoulders as a shawl when the weather turns colder or tie it around your head during unexpected showers – and you can even sit on it if you need to.

551 STUCK IN THE MUD

While strappy sandals may go perfectly with your dress, think about how they will cope on grass if the event is outdoors, especially if it's a little muddy. Go for a more structured heel or wedges so you don't sink into the ground.

552 WEAR A HAT TO BANISH BAD HAIR

Dirty hair is always a problem on camping holidays and at outdoor festivals, so make sure you pack a great summer hat to keep it hidden. Choose a straw cowboy hat or a floppy hat during the day, then swap it for a dark-coloured beanie in the evening.

553 A DAY AT THE RACES

Dressing up for the races is essential, but remember to keep your choices elegant and ladylike. If you'd wear it out to a nightclub or a formal ball, it's not the right choice!

554 KEEP YOUR HEAD DOWN

Although hats are traditionally worn at the races, you don't want to ruin other people's day by blocking the view. Bigger isn't always better! Pill-box hats with netting are a fashionable and chic alternative.

555 PICK ONE FABULOUS ITEM

For those on a budget, work your look around one amazing item such as a hat, shoes or a dress that flatters your best feature and keep everything else low-key.

556 DON'T DAZZLE THE HORSES!

It's important to remember that races are held in the daytime, so make sure you choose a fitting material. Beading and satin can look too much for the day, so go for pretty chiffon or cotton summer dresses instead.

meet & greets

557 IMPRESSING THE IN-LAWS

Whether it's the first time you meet them or the twentieth, save the revealing outfits for your partner and cover up for his parents. You don't need to change your style, just check whether all that flesh really needs to be on show before you leave the house!

558 AFTERNOON TEA

Embrace your inner lady and dress up for afternoon tea parties, which are back in fashion. Go for the traditional flowery tea dresses or A-line skirts and pussy-cat bow blouses. Finish off the look with pastel-coloured pumps, Mary Janes or T-bar heels.

559 DON'T FLASH THE FLESH

You can press the flesh but don't flash it! Social get-togethers are meant to be respectable and are useful for networking, so keep the cleavage covered up.

560 DON'T BE BOLD

Avoid flashy or aggressive colours such as red and black and opt instead for a softer taupe or pewter that will make you appear nonthreatening, calm and approachable. Inject colour with a bright necklace or scarf.

reunions

561 IMPRESS OLD CLASSMATES

The important thing is to feel confident when you dress for a class reunion. Plan ahead so you feel comfortable in what you are wearing. Look through your wardrobe for outfits that you know you look good in, then add up-to-the-minute accessories.

562 RING THE CHANGES

While a new outfit doesn't need to be cutting edge, it should show that you're up to date with changing styles. The best route is to mix a classic with a high fashion item.

563 DRESS YOUR AGE

While you want to look gorgeous for your 'friends or classmates reunited' get-together, don't dress too young – even if you last saw these people 25 years ago! Skintight or too short will look ridiculous; besides, you want them to see how you've grown into a sophisticated, successful adult.

564 BE PREPARED

Go that extra mile when you're seeing people for the first time in years. Every outfit looks better with a well-groomed body so get your hair and nails done, and your eyebrows waxed or threaded.

seasonal holidays

565 ALLOW FOR EXTRA PUD

Avoid the belly bulge after Christmas dinner by wearing tops or dresses that skim over your stomach and have plenty of give so you can comfortably enjoy that extra mince pie.

566 KEEP IT UNDER WRAPS

The annual work Christmas party is a good chance to show your true style, but don't give the wrong impression. Although it's a party, it is still work related so don't ruin your chances of a promotion by exposing too much flesh. Keep it fun and think glamorous but mysterious.

567 BE A STAR

Even if you haven't got hoards of people coming over for Christmas day, it's still good to make an effort. Save a special outfit or new dress and don't be afraid to sparkle. For a fun day you could theme it and ask your guests to all wear a certain colour such as red – this always makes for great photos!

568 AVOID FESTIVE FAUX PAS

If you're acting as hostess for Christmas dinner, be sure to glam it up while still keeping things practical. You are bound to be on your feet quite often so swap your heels for jewelled or satin flats and keep your sleeves three-quarter length so they don't end up trailing in the gravy.

569 DANCING QUEEN

New Year's Eve only happens once a year so make sure you look your best. There's bound to be some dancing involved so go for a stunning dress that lets you move easily and twirl around freely.

570 GREET NEW YEAR ON YOUR FEET

A New Year's Eve party usually involves a long evening on your feet, so make sure your shoes are comfy. Of course you still want to look glamorous with a pair of heels – but they don't have to be your highest pair. You want to be able to dance and not worry about falling over after a few glasses of champagne!

571 PERFECT PINS

The last evening of the year is all about having fun so do the same with your clothes. You could contrast a block-colour dress with brightly coloured tights – or if you are feeling brave, try teaming a black dress with a pair of bright red or purple tights.

572 SPARKLE AND SHINE

Sparkly or sequined dresses or skirts are a perfect Christmas evening look. Team them with a black polo neck so as not to look too overdressed.

travel fashion

573 SET THE SCENE

Good packing is all in the planning. Be realistic about what you need – consider the climate, how long you will be away and exactly what kind of holiday it's going to be.

574 DOWNSIZE YOUR PURSE

You don't need to take your normal purse with its backlog of receipts, reminders and photos on holiday. Treat yourself to a new, minimal wallet that will fit your money and the necessary cards inside, allowing more space in your bag for souvenirs.

575 ADOPT A THEME

Pack clothes that you can mix and match rather than items that only go with one outfit. This will save on packing space and also on washing when you get back. To avoid creasing, layer each outfit as flat as possible with tissue paper between the folds to limit creases, and in order of what you think you might wear first.

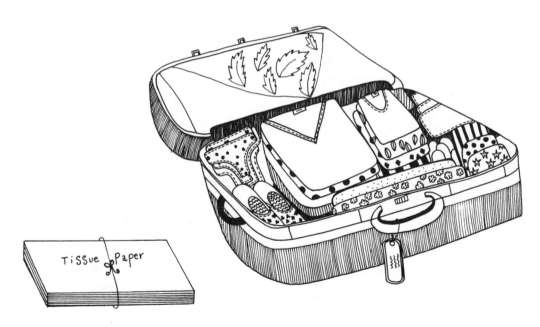

TiSSue Paper

576 CHECK THE WEATHER

It sounds obvious but check the weather forecast for the place you are visiting on the Internet before you pack so that you have an idea of what to expect. Ask your travel agent for the average temperature and rainfall for the time of year you're going, too.

577 CROSS YOUR HEART

An across-the-body handbag is a much more practical choice than a shoulder bag when you're on holiday. Not only does it free up your hands, it will also deter pickpockets – a huge problem in lots of tourist destinations.

578 PASSPORT POWER

Apart from the tickets, your passport is the most important thing about your trip, so give it a well-deserved makeover with a special passport cover. Choose a leather case in a colour that coordinates with your handbag to get your holiday off to a stylish start.

579 STEAM CLEAN

If your clothes are crumpled after being in your suitcase, hang them up in the bathroom while you have a shower and the steam will make the creases disappear effortlessly. For wrinkled jumpers, aim a hot hairdryer at the creases and they will soon drop out.

580 BAG IT UP

Pack your delicate underwear in lingerie bags and keep each pair of shoes in a separate shoebag. Not only will this help your packing be organized, but you will protect your lingerie and keep it from getting tangled up with other items of clothing.

581 STREAMLINE YOUR SUITCASE

A couple of days before your trip, lay out the clothes you want to take and look through them carefully. Often you can downsize the amount you have at the start by a third or even half.

582 BE PREPARED

Pack a spare set of underwear and socks into your hand luggage just in case your suitcase goes missing.

583 MAKE LIKE A LOCAL

Be sure to respect local customs on clothing when visiting countries of different cultures, and pack accordingly. For example, if you're travelling to a Muslim country or plan to visit lots of churches and religious buildings, wear below-the-knee dresses or trousers and have a scarf or shawl handy to cover up your shoulders.

584 DEVELOP SUITCASE CHIC

Battered old luggage will let you down. Look for cases made of good-quality material in stylish colours that coordinate with your outfit.

585 DRESS UP FOR THE PLANE

On the plane, wear your heaviest clothes such as jeans, boots and an overcoat to save much-needed space in your suitcase.

586 PLANE-CLOTHED

Make sure you wear comfortable clothing on your flight, especially for longer journeys. Planes are often colder than you expect, so think layers and take a pair of cosy cashmere socks. Check that your shoes are not too tight as your feet may swell due to the cabin pressure, and pack a pashmina, which you can use instead of scratchy plane blankets.

587 CASE-SHARE

If you are going away with friends, check what they are packing. You may be able to borrow each others' clothes and designate certain items to pack to one another so that you don't end up with four hairdryers and four bottles of shampoo plus conditioner.

588 GET SOME SHUT-EYE

If you have an overnight flight, treat yourself to a pretty eye mask that will assist you in getting a stylish forty winks on the plane and a rested, fresh complexion when you land.

hot-weather holidays

589 ALL THAT GLITTERS

Gold looks fantastic against a great tan so pack some gold jewellery or clothes for a sexy Latino look that maximizes tanned skin and sun-glistened hair.

590 NO SWEAT

If you're going to a hot climate, be sure to pack clothes made of natural fibres that allow your skin to breathe. A pair of floaty cotton trousers or a kaftan will not only cover up bits of your body you are not confident about but will also feel cool and comfortable.

591 PACK BY NUMBERS

For a week's beach break you really only need to pack: two bikinis; two sundresses; a pair of light trousers; a pair of shoes each for the plane, the evening and the day; three or four tops; a sarong; a lightweight sweater or cardigan; and two skirts. Easy – and you'll have lots of room left for duty-free and souvenirs!

592 DRESS IT UP

For a summer holiday always pack a couple of versatile sundresses that you can slip on over a swimsuit, wear for sightseeing during the day, and then smarten up with some jewellery and little heels in the evening.

593 THE RIGHT SHADES

Sunglasses are an essential – but with so many shapes, sizes and colours on offer it's worth spending a bit of time to find the perfect pair. Ask a friend to give you their honest opinion. And make sure your shades protect against UVB and UVA rays. Photochromic lenses protects the eyes from glare, sun and UV radiation, and don't distort colour.

594 STOP SANDALS BEING A FLOP

Give your flip-flops a test run before packing them – not all flip-flops are created equal. If you are going on a beach holiday, they will be the staple of your day wear and you don't want to be hobbling around with blisters on day one.

595 WET SUITS

Take separate swim bags to keep swimsuits and bikinis in – especially if you might have to carry them about when they're wet. Pack a small sachet of detergent to rinse them in to prevent chlorine or salt build-up over the holiday period.

596 ENJOY A SHOE SPREE

If you find the perfect flip-flops, it's worth stocking up on a few pairs. Flip-flops can look worn and grubby very quickly so by having a number of styles you can alternate they'll last longer too.

597 WISE BUYS?

When purchasing clothes abroad, stop to think about whether you will actually wear them back home, away from the sun and exotic atmosphere of your holiday. The chances are you probably won't.

598 SARONG STAR

Pack at least one sarong if you're going on a beach holiday. Even if you don't wear it on the beach, it can be used as a towel and it take up hardly any room in your suitcase.

599 PALE AND INTERESTING

Save your light-coloured bikinis and white dresses for the last few days of your holiday when you have built up more of a tan, otherwise they may leave you looking washed-out in the bright sun.

600 GOOD SUPPORT

Padded bikinis are not only fantastic for offering support on the beach but can also double up as bras for the evening, saving you valuable space in your suitcase.

601 ROMAN HOLIDAY

Keep your basic flip-flops for the beach and look for smarter sandals for the evening. The gladiator sandal is a stylish alternative that will look fabulous with a tan and dress and equally good with trousers or shorts.

602 MAXED-OUT

Long summer maxi-dresses are great for an effortless boho look in the evenings. Choose styles with thin straps to show off your tanned shoulders and back.

603 COSY CASHMERE

On cooler evenings, cashmere sweaters are the perfect solution. Stylish and cosy, they offer a lightweight yet warm solution for summer breezes. They might be more expensive but it's worth paying a little extra as they'll last for years.

604 SHOW SOME LEG

When you're running about sightseeing, loose linen shorts are great for looking stylish and feeling cool. And you'll still get a tan on your legs without having to lie on the beach.

605 TONE IT DOWN

If you've over-done the sun, avoid wearing bright colours, which will highlight your red, burning skin. Stick to pale shades and use a cardigan or pashmina to cover sunburnt shoulders.

606 LESS IS MORE

Save your best accessories for the evening. A few thin gold or leather bracelets are fine for daywear, but putting on all your bling for the beach will look as if you're trying too hard.

607 JOIN THE COTTON CLUB

Invest in a flattering pair of linen trousers before your holiday. Not only are they great for beach holidays but you can wear them on city breaks with strappy vests and pretty summer shirts.

608 COVERED TO A T

If your shoulders are prone to burning, keep a couple of T-shirts in your bag that you can throw on at the beach or while sightseeing to protect your skin.

609 SUNCREAM SAVVY

Even when you're in a rush to get out and about during the day, make sure your sun cream or aftersun is dry before dressing to avoid getting marks on your clothing.

610 COLOURED UP

Be brave with colour. If you always wear darker shades at home, a sunny location offers the perfect opportunity to experiment with bright shades without feeling as if you're standing out too much from the crowd. Bold colour looks fantastic against tanned skin.

611 FIFTIES CHIC

Look stylish on the beach and protect your hair with a floppy sun hat that you can team with 1950s-inspired glasses for the ultimate Grace Kelly glamour look.

612 EARLY BIRD

If you plan to go away in the summer, start stocking up on summer clothes from the beginning of spring. Most of the really good items will have been snapped up by mid-summer so by getting in early not only will you get the best pickings, but you won't be spending lots of money just before your trip on last-minute panic buys.

cold-weather holidays

613 SKI IN STYLE

Ski-wear doesn't have to be dull. Many designers are turning the ski slopes into catwalks with their own collections. Though expensive, they are often made of high-quality material and have a high performance level. If you can't afford the whole get-up, invest in accessories, which are more affordable.

614 LAYER IT ON THICK

If you are going on a winter city break, packing layers – such as long-sleeved T-shirts, cashmere cardigans and pashminas – is the best way to ensure you stay warm without having to take your biggest, heaviest sweaters.

615 HOT LEGS

Embrace your inner 1980s child with a pair of leg-warmers to keep warm on winter holidays. Go for interesting colours and patterns if you want to make a statement or dark colours for a more grown-up look. Wear them over skinny jeans and knee-high boots.

616 LOVE IN A COLD CLIMATE

If your man has taken you on a romantic mini-break during the winter months, don't just think about what to wear for cocktails in the evening; pack at least one cosy but cute walking outfit. Think something chic but sturdy that wouldn't look out of place when you're strolling through a frosty, tree-lined park.

617 STATEMENT ON THE SLOPES

On skiing holidays, one of the best ways to show off your sense of style is by choosing striking hats and up-to-the-minute sunglasses.

618 CHOOSE COATS WITH CARE

For winter city breaks, a warm and fabulous coat is a must. It's your one chance to exude style while the rest of your clothes are covered up. Choose a striking scarf, hat and glove combo for extra fashion points.

619 LONG ICED-TS

On a winter vacation, take a variety of long-sleeved T-shirts in various bright colours. They are incredibly versatile and can be worn under short-sleeved tops, sweaters or the jacket of a suit.

city & weekend breaks

620 TRY A TUNIC

A tunic dress is an ideal item of clothing to take on a weekend break, as it's so versatile. Wear it over skinny jeans in the daytime and then with tights and heels for an evening out.

621 SAVE SPACE

If you plan to visit cities and are set on a spot of retail therapy, make sure you pack lightly so you have plenty of room for new clothes on the return trip.

622 WEEKEND WARDROBE

For weekends away, aim for a capsule wardrobe that is easy to coordinate – and light to carry! Two dresses, one pair of trousers, two tops and a light sweater should be plenty. You can add accessories at night for colour and style.

623 CITY CHIC

Instead of trousers, check out smart city shorts that will look great teamed with a pretty top and scarf on a sunny mini-break.

624 GO FLAT-HUNTING

Comfortable shoes are a must for weekend and city breaks filled with sightseeing. Flat ballet-style pumps look great and are very practical. Wear new shoes around the house for a few days before your trip so you don't get blisters.

625 DITCH THE SUITCASE

If you're only going away for a couple of days, pack all your items in a small suitcase to carry as hand luggage. By doing this you can spend less time waiting at the airport and more time enjoying your trip.

626 DEAL WITH DIFFERENT TEMPERATURES

Pack a cotton long-sleeved top in your bag for walking around warm foreign cities so you can cover up while visiting chillier air-conditioned buildings or churches.

pregnancy fashion

627 DRESS YOUR BUMP WITH STYLE

Being pregnant does not mean you can't be stylish. Smock tops and dresses are perfect for incorporating growing bumps while still looking pretty and chic.

628 PUT YOUR FEET UP

When you're pregnant, the last thing you want to do is haul yourself around shops to find clothes. Do this from the comfort of your own home. There are dozens of great maternity-wear websites that deliver gorgeous pregnancy outfits direct to your door.

629 GET SOME LAYERS

Try layering simple camisoles with chiffon over tops in accompanying colours for a chic and pretty look that will keep you cool on summer days while flattering your bump.

630 BALANCE IT OUT

Because the tops you will be wearing have to 'grow', avoid feeling like you're wearing a tent by ensuring your bottom half is more streamlined. Look for slim-legged pregnancy jeans to minimize your overall volume.

631 PRETTY FLATS

With swollen ankles and that extra baby weight, cute flat shoes are a must for pregnant women. Treat yourself to a couple of pairs in different fabrics so you can wear them to formal and informal occasions.

632 WIDTH OVER HEIGHT

There's no health reason why you can't wear heels from time to time, but with the extra baby weight, be kind to tired feet and go for sturdy heels that offer more support.

633 HEAD-TO-TOE COLOUR

To look smart while pregnant, an easy option is to wear one colour from top to bottom, which will also make you appear smaller than might feel!

634 SHOW OFF YOUR SLIM BITS

If you are pregnant but haven't put on much
weight anywhere else, don't be afraid to
display your best features such as shoulders
and arms in off-the-shoulder dresses. Being
pregnant doesn't mean you can't look sexy.
Quite the opposite, in fact.

635 BUY ONE SIZE UP

Maternity clothes aren't compulsory in
the early months, especially if it's only
your tummy that's grown – just buy a
size bigger. You can then wear the same
stretchy dresses, tops and shirts after the
birth while losing your baby weight.

636 SAY NO TO FRILLS AND FUSS

You'll feel bulky on your top half, so don't
add to it with overly fussy tops. Keep detail
to a minimum and go for chic, simple lines.

637 BE BIAS

Dresses cut on the bias will have more give
than straight-cut styles and are the perfect
choice when your bump is getting bigger.

638 DRESS UP YOUR JOGGING BOTTOMS

While you may previously have worn your jogging bottoms only to the gym, they're a comfy option for pregnant women. But this doesn't mean they have to look scruffy. Look in sports shops for black yoga pants that are made from good-quality material, which you can team with a crisp white shirt.

639 WORKING MUM

Looking chic in the office while pregnant can become a challenge. To make it easy, create a capsule wardrobe with a pair of smart trousers with an elasticated or drawstring waistband, a skirt, a jacket you can wear open, a dress and a tunic top. They can be mixed and matched to create different looks and should see you through in style.

640 STICK TO YOUR FAVOURITE STORES

Being pregnant doesn't mean you should avoid the shops you love best. Many of the major high-street stores have fantastic maternity collections mirroring up-to-the-minute trends.

641 THINK BEFORE YOU BUY

There will probably be a few things in your wardrobe that you can continue to wear throughout the pregnancy with a little alteration. For example, wear your favourite cardigans and shirts open with a long camisole top underneath.

642 CAPE CRUSADER

Instead of investing in an expensive maternity coat that you won't wear once you have given birth, keep warm and fashionable with dark-coloured ponchos or capes that fall below your bottom.

643 SHOW OFF YOUR CURVES

V-neck tops and scoop-neck tops in empire lines will flatter an ever-growing cleavage and prevent you from looking large on top.

644 SOFT ON SKIN

During pregnancy your skin can be extra-sensitive and you will be prone to hot flushes. Avoid man-made fabrics that might irritate and think about layering so you can alter your temperature easily.

645 ADD STYLE WITH ACCESSORIES

Accessories are great for mums-to-be – earrings, scarves, bangles and shoes generally still fit, no matter how much you've grown! They will also smarten up an otherwise relaxed outfit.

646 GET SOME SUPPORT

Your bust will grow at least a cup size when pregnant so it's important to get bras that fit your size and offer great support – your local department store should be able to help. And remember to have yourself measured properly for a nursing bra just a few weeks before the birth if you plan to breastfeed.

647 SOME EXTRA STRETCH

One sneaky trick that will allow you to carry on wearing your favourite pair of trousers in the first few months of pregnancy is to loop an elastic band through the button-hole and hook it around the button. Make sure you disguise it by wearing a long shirt over the top, though.

648 TRY THE BUM AND TUM TEST

Before your bump is developed enough to fill out maternity clothes, you can still get away with wearing clothes in your existing wardrobe so long as the clothes are long enough to cover your tummy and hang to a safe length beneath your butt.

649 FREE AND EASY

It's important to make sure your clothes have extra stretch so they won't burst at the seams. Avoid restricted materials and choose ones with extra give such as jersey, soft knits, cotton and viscose.

650 SORT OUT SIZING

Always select your pre-pregnancy size when buying maternity clothes. After all, your arms and legs don't get longer and your basic body structure will remain the same. Well-made maternity garments adjust for pregnancy, giving you extra room only where you need it – belly, bust and hips – while maintaining the pre-pregnancy proportions of each size range.

651 DON'T GO WITH THE FLOW

While many pregnant women think that their only dress option is big and floaty, this can often make them look even bigger. Instead, show off your new-found curves in more fitted clothes. They don't have to be supertight, but dresses with a ruched front or sides will be more flattering while still being comfortable.

652 HANG LOW

When your bump is small, rather than buying pregnancy jeans that you'll never wear again, look in your favourite stores for low-cut jeans that do up under the belly which you can still wear after the birth. You could even cut the waistband off existing jeans to give you more room – and save money.

653 SOMETHING BORROWED ...

Who wants to spend money on clothes they may never wear again? Instead of paying out for a whole pregnancy wardrobe, borrow items from friends who have already had their babies or hunt for bargains in charity shops.

654 BEAUTIFULLY WRAPPED

Wrap-around dresses and tops are a great choice for soon-to-be mums as the v-neck front will flatter your chest and the tied waist allows for the growth of your bump. Choose one or two sizes bigger than you normally are to allow for give.

655 PERFECT PRINTS

Just because you are pregnant, it doesn't mean you should be afraid to wear colour or pattern. So many women stick to dark colours during pregnancy but going for bright-coloured long tops or dresses will make you stand out from the crowd and stop you feeling dowdy.

656 RECYCLE OLD TROUSERS

Most women have a couple of pairs of linen trousers or cargo pants lurking in their wardrobes from the summer so instead of buying new trousers, reuse these. If the waistbands aren't drawstring, leave the waistband undone and loop a thick belt over the top. Team with a long cotton top.

657 MAKE LIKE A CELEBRITY

You won't catch star mums looking anything other than über-stylish when they're pregnant. They tend to customize their normal clothes, often just buying in a bigger size.

658 CREAM OF THE CROP

Although skirts may be an easy option for pregnant women, trousers are often slightly more practical. Capri pants and knee-length shorts can be smart, sassy alternatives and also keep you cool.

659 SHOW OFF YOUR SHAPE

Define your figure by choosing long floaty tops with ties that do up under the bust or at the side. For glamorous evening events, add a thick ribbon or a belt to shapeless tops under the bust and above the bump.

660 BUTTON IT UP

Shirtdresses that have a panelled front or pleating at the back for extra 'give' are great options to wear to work or for smart occasions, especially early on in your pregnancy when your bump is still small.

661 TAKE INSPIRATION FROM OTHER COUNTRIES

Being pregnant gives you the chance to experiment with your new body shape. Look to other cultures to see what pregnant women wear. Consider African-inspired long skirts or Thai fishermen's trousers that fit all sizes.

662 GET GOOD COVER

Short-sleeved cardigans and cowls that hang loosely to the waist are great for keeping you warm on summer evenings and flattering your bump.

gym & sportswear

663 AND STRETCH ...

Gym clothes should allow you to move freely. Look for materials that have some extra stretch in them so you don't feel restricted and unable to twist into that tricky yoga pose!

664 YOGA MATTERS

By spending a bit extra on well-made and flattering yoga bottoms, not only will you look good in class, but you can also wear them for a stylish yet relaxed look around the house.

665 GO DESIGNER

Although it may seem ridiculous to splash out on clothes you are just going to sweat in, designer sportswear will give you extra style and support. Some designers have their own ranges at department stores and big sports brands such as Nike or Adidas are available at more affordable prices. Watch out, too, for sales.

666 AVOID SWEAT MARKS

Minimize sweat marks by looking out for specially designed sports clothes that are made of 'wicking' fabric, such as high-tech polyester, which draws sweat away from the body. While items made of this breathable fabric are a little more expensive, they'll keep you comfortable and dry.

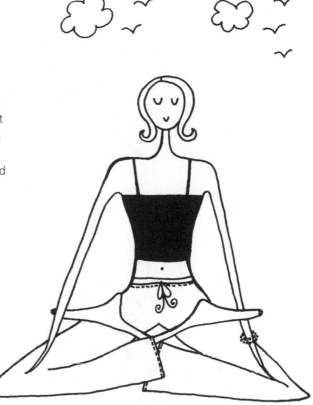

667 USE LAYERS

If you're exercising outside, the best way to deal with changes in body temperature is thin layers. A strappy vest under a thin long-sleeved top with a thin zip-up means you can add or discard items as you go.

668 GIVE GREY THE SLIP

Grey clothes are notable for showing up unflattering sweat patches, so leave tops in this shade behind when doing cardio exercises and stick to black or red instead.

669 DON'T GO BUST

The right bra is essential for exercising, especially if your breasts are big. Go to a sports shop to find a well-designed bra that will lift, hold and separate. Opt for feel over look – bouncing, unsupported boobs are uncomfortable and bad for your back.

670 PLAY UP YOUR BEST BITS

Just because you're going to the gym, this doesn't mean that you shouldn't highlight your favourite body parts. If you already have great abs, go for tops that show them, or reveal well-toned legs by wearing shorts.

671 SECRET SUPPORT

Built-in support on vest tops in well-designed fitness clothing means you can show off toned arms and shoulders while keeping everything else in place.

672 IT ONLY TAKES TWO

Having at least two great-looking gym outfits that flatter your figure and make you feel good will give you extra incentive to go to the gym and show off your sleek, chic look.

673 GYM BAG CHIC

Don't throw all your fashionable gym clothes into a tired old satchel, and especially not a plastic bag. Look for well-made and stylish bags that make you feel fabulous from the moment you head to the gym until the minute you get home.

674 PLAY IT SAFE IN BLACK

Black is the most flattering of colours and great to wear to the gym if you feel self-conscious about your figure. Add some colour by choosing black trousers with piping or waistbands in a different shade.

675 DON'T FORGET TO ACCESSORIZE

Just because you're working out doesn't mean you can't wear cool accessories. Forget jewellery and try coloured sweatbands or hair bands to keep your hair out of your eyes.

676 A GOOD FIT

A big mistake that many women make in the gym is to wear overly baggy clothes – but this actually makes them look larger. The most flattering fitness clothes are those that follow the shape of your body and give you a waist.

677 PICK THE RIGHT PANTIES

When exercising, your main consideration should be comfort. Choose underwear that you know is comfortable and won't ride up or sneak out on show. Give thongs a miss unless you are going to be wearing tight leggings and want to avoid VPL.

678 TREAT YOUR FEET

Don't ruin a stylish gym look with battered old trainers (sneakers). Treat yourself to a new pair that flatter your feet, but think too about what you need them for. For example, you'll require more support in trainers for jogging than in the shoes you wear to Pilates class.

679 PROTECT YOUR EYES

Don't forget a pair of sunglasses to avoid straining your eyes when exercising in the sun. Protection is essential when sailing, playing tennis or when exercising on the beach. Make sure sunglasses sit snugly on your face and choose sleek and stylish ones that stay in place, over big and glamorous, for when you're working out.

680 DRESS UP FOR TENNIS

Make like you're at Wimbledon and dress up for your matches in tennis dresses and skirts. Wear suitable underwear or shorts underneath to protect your modesty and select dresses that give support on the top half plus freedom to move your legs easily.

681 KEEP MUSCLES WARM

When you first arrive at the gym and later while you are cooling down, throw on a stylish zip-up or wrap-around top. Choose one with some colour and in a material that matches the rest of your gym-wear.

682 SHOW OFF SPORTS TOPS

If you've splashed out on a well-made and stylish sports top that you love, there's no reason why you can't wear it casually, too. It's ideal for daytime walks or summer picnics teamed with the right shorts or skirt.

SHOPPING

planning ahead

683 PLAN AHEAD

Review your wardrobe the morning before you go shopping to remind yourself of what you already have and any holes that need filling. Yes, you may love them all but it's no good having ten pairs of black trousers and five beige cardies if you've nothing to go with them!

684 WRITE A LIST

Before you go out shopping for clothes write down a list of exactly what you're looking for – and stick to it. This will save you money because you won't be distracted by other items that you don't really need.

685 TEAR IT UP

Every time you see a garment you love in a magazine, rip it out – even if it's just an overall look you admire. Keep in your handbag for instant inspiration when you're out shopping.

686 FIRST THINGS FIRST

Make a list of 'must visit' shops and stick to it. Knowing exactly where you want to go stops you wasting time and energy in so-so shops.

687 WORK YOUR WARDROBE

Be it a coat, a pair of brown boots or a top to go with that skirt you've never found a match for, make a list of exactly what you need. Think about pieces that will make your wardrobe work better – a versatile belt, cream scarf, tailored shirt, etc.

688 FIX YOUR PRICE

Set a limit on how much you can spend and be firm: do not allow yourself to go over that figure. If you know you can't control yourself once you see something you like, leave your credit and store cards at home. Try taking cash instead, as it feels more 'real'. It's also a lot harder to hand over crisp notes than a piece of plastic and this will really test whether you want that new dress as much as you think!

689 THERE'S NO RUSH

Allow plenty of time. Shopping when you are in a hurry or thinking about all the other things you have to do is a bad idea. You'll only end up rushing and buying something in haste that you will almost certainly hate once you've got it home.

690 TAKE IT WITH YOU

If you have a skirt that you love but have never found anything to wear it with, or maybe a top that none of your bottoms quite match, pop it in a bag and take it out shopping. Make it your mission to find the perfect partner.

691 PANIC BUYS

Don't go shopping for an outfit for an important occasion the day before the event. If you can't find what you want, you'll end up panic-buying or getting hot and flustered because you can't find what you like. Have a dry run a couple of weeks beforehand, then go for the proper shop when you have a clearer idea of what you really want.

692 BE A LONE BROWSER

Shopping on your own is quicker and you won't get sidetracked. If you really need a second opinion, you can always try the garment on at home and ask someone but make sure the shop offers returns first.

693 TAKE A TOOL KIT

Pack hair clips and a pair of heels when you go shopping so you can get an idea of different ways to wear dresses and trousers.

694 PRIORITIZE PURCHASES

What's the most important purchase you want to make? If you won't feel satisfied unless you go home with the perfect coat, don't allow yourself to be distracted by other items until you've found it.

695 GET YOUR UNDIES RIGHT

Go shopping in the lingerie you expect to wear under the outfit you're buying. It's no good wearing a red bra and panties if you're out looking for a cream cotton summer dress. Similarly, take a pair of tights if you intend to try on a new skirt or dress.

696 HAVE A 'SHOPPING' OUTFIT

Wear clothes that are easy to take on and off without making you look like a rumpled mess by the end of the day. Streamlined but supportive underwear won't spoil the look of any clothes you try on. And do your hair and make-up so you see yourself in the best light.

sensible shopping

697 AVOID RETAIL AS THERAPY

Don't shop when you're feeling down. You will end up buying mistake items or being overcritical of yourself – both of which can make you feel worse. See a film, take some exercise or meet a friend for lunch for a more effective pick-me-up.

698 THREE CRUCIAL QUESTIONS

Ask yourself these three questions before you buy anything. Does it fit? Will it go with what I already have? And does it suit me?

699 JUST SAY NO

If you're going shopping with a friend after a big lunch, restrict yourself to mineral water. Many a disastrous fashion choice has been made after a glass of Pinot!

700 JUST WON'T WASH?

Check the washing instructions on the label. Does the item seem quite so desirable if you're going to have to hand-wash or dry-clean it after every wear?

701 WHEN I'M THINNER ...

Don't put off making wardrobe choices until you lose weight – choose pieces that can camouflage problem areas instead.

702 DOUBLE UP

If you find some trousers or a skirt that's the perfect fit, consider buying more than one, especially if they are black. While black tends to fade after a time, with two pairs of the same trousers the wear and tear takes longer.

703 DON'T GET STUCK IN A RUT

While it's good to know what suits you, don't let this stop you from being adventurous from time to time and trying new styles and colours. Otherwise, you'll end up feeling as if you're wearing a uniform.

704 VARY THE VENUE

Even if you absolutely adore the range in a certain store, buy from other shops too. Otherwise, you'll start to look as if you work for them.

705 BUY FOR NOW

While shops change their ranges more quickly, catalogues tend to hold stock for longer, which means you can often buy clothes in season that you can wear now instead of months ahead. This helps if you find it hard to imagine how you'll feel in that floaty summer dress on a cold spring morning!

in the changing room

706 BE REALISTIC

Just because it looks great on the shop assistant, this doesn't mean it will look equally good on you. She could have an entirely different body shape and colouring – so always try things on before buying and make sure they suit your frame and hair and skin tones.

707 GIVE YOURSELF A 360

Always check the fit of what you are about to buy in a three-way mirror so you can see yourself from every angle. This prevents you getting a nasty surprise when you catch a glimpse of your backside in a shop window at some point in the future!

708 UP A LEVEL

Go up a size or two – psychologically we hate moving up from the size we normally wear but sometimes it can actually make a fabric drape better, especially across the bottom and hips.

709 BE A FASHION FRIEND

If you're shopping with a friend and she asks your opinion about the orange leopard-print leggings she's trying on, be honest with her. You'll both regret it if she gets home and hates them.

710 GET THE LIGHT RIGHT

Don't be afraid to ask if you can take a garment out to a natural light source to check what it looks like in daylight. Artificial lighting can change the colour of clothes dramatically.

711 SIT IT OUT

Always sit down in an item of clothing when trying it on. What may fit while standing can pull or gape open once you sit down and ruin the shape of a garment completely.

712 WALK THIS WAY

Take a walk in your outfit before you buy it. Many skirts and dresses can look perfect when you are standing still, only to ride up once you walk along. The waistband of your skirt should be large enough so that it doesn't pucker or roll up.

713 MIRROR, MIRROR ...

Beware of those misleading 'skinny' mirrors in department stores and boutiques. If a style didn't look good on you in the past, it won't now – unless you've made some major changes to your diet and exercise regime.

getting a good fit

714 DON'T SQUEEZE IN

When buying jackets and coats, remember that the sleeves should just hit the wrist bone and the fabric mustn't cling to or stretch over any problem areas.

715 FOLLOW YOUR BODY

As a general rule, clothes look best when they skim your silhouette. Pieces so tight that you can see every bone and muscle will make you seem heavy; too loose and baggy and you'll look shapeless, not slim.

716 RIGHT FOR YOU

Forget about fashion – find the hem length that's most flattering to you and stick with it! Stand in front of a full-length mirror in an 'average' shoe. Hold a piece of fabric in front of you and raise it to different heights on your leg. Notice where your leg looks thicker or thinner, and never choose a skirt length that hits your leg at the fullest part. You may suit two or three skirts length but you'll need to take other heel heights into consideration.

717 HEEL, GIRL!

Trouser bottoms should rest about 2.5 cm (1 in) above the heel and the hems should sit slightly bent on the top of your feet – have one 'break' in the crease. If you're wearing high heels, trousers should be longer to account for the extra height.

718 SOCK IT TO 'EM

Often people forget that different outfits
require different socks. Invest in a variety of
colours and thicknesses to go under your
trousers and shoes. Pop socks, for example,
are great if you're wearing a long skirt or
ballet pumps – which many socks are too
thick to wear with. Over-the-knee socks
are perfect in winter as they're warm and
add an extra layer over tights or bare legs.
They're best worn with shorter skirts but
can also be teamed with heels or boots.

719 BE KIND TO BUTTONS

Buttons look terrible under strain so make
sure that you can do up those on coats,
shirts and cardigans, even if you intend to
wear them open. The garment will look
odd if it doesn't do what's intended.

720 PICK A PRO

Ask the sales assistant in a reputable
store to find you clothes that fit – it is
their job after all. They should be able to
recommend the correct size for you in
their brand.

721 GET THE BENDS

Make sure you can bend your arms without difficulty when you try on tops and jackets. Bend your knees, too. Anything too tight or chafing will hurt you and also damage the clothing.

722 MADE TO MEASURE

Many shop-bought jackets are too wide across the shoulders. A good tailor or seamstress should be able to take them in from the centre seam to fit you perfectly.

723 KEEP YOUR TROUSERS ON

Check that any new trousers don't have too much fabric in the zipper and crotch – this can make them bunch unattractively.

724 HONEY, I'VE SHRUNK MY SWEATER

Make sure when you buy pure wool cardigans or sweaters that they're ever so slightly too big for you. When you wash them, no matter how careful you may be, there will always be some shrinkage. Buy shrewdly and they'll fit you perfectly after the first wash.

725 CH-CH-CH-CHANGES

Invest in good alterations if something doesn't fit or if you lose or gain weight – clothing that doesn't fit properly will never leave your wardrobe.

726 SKIRT LENGTHS

Skirts look best when they hit just above or just below the knees. But avoid shin-length skirts because they tend to make most people appear shorter and bow-legged.

727 TIGHT FIT

The only way to make sure tights fit is to try them on. If this isn't practical, go for larger rather than smaller sizes or they'll hang too low between your legs and you might ladder them while trying to pull them on.

728 UP YOUR SLEEVE

Jacket sleeves should be slim to show off the shape of the arms but loose enough to allow you to wear a thin sweater underneath. The bottom of the jacket must hit the hipbones – any shorter or longer tends to make people look squat and bulky.

729 BESPOKE IS SOMETIMES BEST

Even couture-fitted dresses sometimes gape (take a look at the stars on the red carpet at the Oscars!) so ensure a neat fit by paying a bit more. Have a dress made-to-measure for a special occasion or arrange for a tailor to alter it to fit. Many shops now offer their own fitting service.

730 TUCK IT IN

A good tailored shirt should fit neatly around your torso and be long enough to tuck in – and stay tucked in. Don't buy shirts that scrimp on fabric at the bottom: you'll only end up looking like an unmade bed as the day goes on.

731 MAKE A COPY

If you find a shirt or skirt that fits you perfectly and really flatters your figure, it's worth visiting a tailor to have it carefully measured so you know your exact size for future reference. It's helpful to keep a note of your size in centimetres as dress sizes vary so much from store to store these days.

732 CREATURE COMFORTS

Clothes should never be too painful to wear! Any garments that cut you in half, give you tummy pains, cut off circulation or make you feel faint should be ditched, no matter how gorgeous or glam. You're damaging your health!

733 AVOID A SQUEEZE

Lycra added to garments is no excuse for you to go a size smaller – jeans and jackets should still fit properly. The elastic simply means that the clothes move with and fit your body more easily and so are more comfortable to wear.

734 THE RIGHT BUTTONS

Check where the buttons sit on your shirt. A good fit means the neck isn't too low or too high and when open-necked, the top button should sit just above the bust.

735 DON'T BE PANTS!

You've bought underwear a size too small if they dig in, leave marks on your flesh or you have a VPL (Visible Panty Line) under trousers or dresses.

getting a bargain

736 STICK TO CLASSICS

That orange and blue miniskirt might be very this season but how will it look this time next year? During sales you're better off sticking to simple, timeless pieces.

737 HAVE A PLAN

Don't just wander around shops hoping that bargains will jump out at you. Instead, target the stores with clothes you love, be methodical and look at everything, and then don't wait to see if there's anything better than that lovely shirt at half price – it might not be there when you return.

738 IS THE PRICE RIGHT?

By law, shops have to display the original price of the item on sale and it has to have been for sale at this price for at least 28 days. If it doesn't have this information, staff are obliged to tell you so you know whether you're really getting a bargain.

739 GIVE IT THE FITNESS TEST

Unless you're great at sewing or can afford a good tailor, only buy things in the right size and that fit you perfectly. The only exceptions are trousers or skirts that simply need taking up in length.

740 SUPERSALE SWAP

If you've managed to buy some disasters in the sales and you can't return them, don't panic. Have a sales swap party and exchange your unwanted bargains with friends.

741 GET HAGGLING

If you're buying a lot of items from one store during the sale, don't be afraid to ask for a discount for paying with cash. Request to speak to the manager, though – assistants don't always have the authority to make reductions.

742 THINK COMFORT

When buying, remember that anything that feels uncomfortable when you first try it on will be murder by the end of the day!

743 BE FIRM

Decide what you're looking for and stick to it. Don't allow yourself to become sidetracked by price cuts. That cheap dress isn't a bargain if you never wear it.

744 THREE IS THE MAGIC NUMBER

If you can't see yourself wearing it on at least three different occasions (unless it's sportswear or a wedding dress of course!), don't buy it!

745 NO SALE

Don't be drawn in by the price in red. To pass the test, it has to fit, go with at least two items in your wardrobe and have the 'wow' factor.

746 THE LITTLE THINGS IN LIFE

Sales are a great time to stock up on belts, scarves and gloves. Buy winter classics in summer (and vice versa) to make sure they last until the next season.

747 ALWAYS ASK FOR HELP

If you can't see the item in your size, it's always worth asking the shop assistant to check the stockroom or phone around other stores to see if they can locate one. Most will send it to the branch you're visiting or even send it direct to you.

748 NET A BARGAIN

Before you shop, check online to see what's on sale in the store to save joining the scrum for nothing! You can even order from the comfort of your armchair to save you that trip into town.

749 IS IT WORTH IT?

Try this value trick. When you're putting on your bargain top or dress, ask yourself if you love it so much that you'd happily pay full price. If the answer's no, think twice before you buy.

750 GET STOCKED UP

At sale time, stock up on basics – cotton panties, socks, tights, white shirts, black trousers, neutral shoes, etc.

751 FEELING BLUE

Many of the big department stores have 'blue cross' sale days where they cut their prices for a few days only. Find out when these dates are due and wait until then to stock up on new clothes on the cheap.

752 BUDGET BOUTIQUES

Those pricy boutique clothing stores that are normally beyond your price range often do amazing reductions on clothes at sale times, frequently cutting prices by more than 70 per cent. You may still be paying normal high street prices but you'll also be buying designer pieces that are longer-lasting and will look fabulous on. Go just before the end of any sale for even more incredible reductions.

753 LUXE LINGERIE FOR LESS

Many of the large department stores have designer underwear that is also reduced during annual sales. Visit on the first few days of the sale when there will be more sizes available – the most common sizes are soon snapped up.

754 DAY TRIPPER

Enjoy a weekend day trip out to one of the large retail outlets or shopping malls scattered across the country. They offer amazing discounts on chain and designer stores so you are guaranteed to come away with a bargain or two. Check the Internet to find the nearest one to where you live.

755 THE PRICE IS RIGHT

If you are buying an item that you know you won't be wearing in a year's time, check out the cheaper high-street shops first – unless a certain trend and style really suits you and you might get more mileage out of it. Often chain stores are perfect for buying up-to-the-minute trends without breaking the bank.

756 CHEAP ISN'T ALWAYS CHEERFUL

Avoid buying sale items in very cheap stores – their clothes are affordable at any time of year. Use the sales to obtain upmarket garments at knockdown prices in shops you can't usually afford.

757 RETURN OF THE MAC

Make sure you check the store's policy on returns at the time of purchase. They all differ and sometimes sale items may vary from regular stock.

758 DESIGNER DISCOUNT

Many designer shops have discount days that they don't always advertise. Keep an eye out on their websites for upcoming events and sign up to any mailing lists.

759 A LITTLE LUXE

Now is the time to buy very high-quality items. Good-quality leather boots, handbags and shoes at sale prices are a great investment and will last for years.

760 MAKE FRIENDS

Get friendly with the assistants in your favourite stores. Buy a couple of pieces at full price to show willing, but if you can't afford that fabulous pair of trousers or to-die-for dress, ask the date of the next sale and keep an eye out for falling prices.

761 DAMAGED GOODS

Just because clothes are in the sale it doesn't mean they can be ripped, stained or have buttons missing. Shops must alert shoppers to damaged goods before they're sold – you can either get a further discount or your money back. Damage does occur during the sale, too, so always keep an eye out.

762 SUPERSIZE ME!

If you're one of the less common sizes, you can really capitalize in the sales. Small shoes sizes and tiny or larger dress sizes tend to be left over, while more average sizes are usually sold out at full price.

763 SHOP AROUND

To avoid spending unnecessary cash, ask shop assistants to hold items that you are interested in while you continue your search. Most will be happy to put clothes on hold until the next day. After a cooling-off period you can objectively decide whether that hot-pink skirt is such a good buy after all.

764 MAKE USE OF OFFERS

Often high-street stores have 'three for two' offers in which you can buy a basic shirt or vest top in bulk at a discount. Take advantage of this to stock up on basics.

money-saving fashion

765 CHARGE IT

Many high street stores offer a 10% or 20% discount when you open an account with them and often have further discounts throughout the year. There's nothing to stop you from opening a store card for the discount then never using it ever again. If you are worried that you might put things on your card only to end up paying high interest rates, leave the card tucked away at home so you won't be tempted.

766 COMBINE CHEAP AND PRICEY

Mix less-expensive sale clothes with more costly accessories to make your whole outfit appear pricier. Buy a bargain dress or suit but spend a bit more on a classy scarf or gorgeous belt. Just changing the buttons on a marked-down shirt can make it look twice the price, too.

767 BE A BRIDGET JONES

Keep a diary and write down every single penny you spend for a month. You'll be astonished at how much goes on nonessentials – lunch, chocolate, lattes, etc. – and it soon adds up. Save cash by taking a packed lunch to work and have up to £100 ($200) extra per month to spend on clothes or shoes!

768 VOUCH FOR IT

Look out for those 15% and 20% money-off vouchers for high-street stores that often come free with magazines. Save serious cash by using them at the beginning of the season when you need to make big purchases such as a coat or pair of boots.

769 DON'T BE A 10% VICTIM

Research shows we only ever wear 10% of our entire wardrobe. So before buying anything new, ask yourself that difficult question: 'Do I really need another pair of shoes or is there something in the unused 90% of my wardrobe that I can fall in love with again?'

770 CUSTOMIZE TO YOUR PERSONALITY

Get a longer lease of life out of your existing clothes by updating them with added embroidery, new ribbon ties or corsages or even by adding on a panel to make a short skirt into a maxi length.

771 WORTH PER WEAR

When it comes to deciding what to buy, think realistically about how often you will wear something. If it's a decision between one expensive item and two cheaper ones, you may find that in reality you end up wearing the more expensive garment more often and actually save yourself more money in the long run, rather than buying cheaper clothes that soon date.

772 SELL, SELL, SELL!

Use eBay and car boot (garage) sales to buy and sell clothes. Some people actually make a living these days from buying and selling online. You can sell almost anything for the price of a small commission. And garage sales are fantastic for making money out of junk – it's amazing what people will buy!

773 USE WEB DISCOUNTS

Sign up to online discount services (such as www.sendmediscounts.co.uk) to learn about discounts currently on offer on a whole range of clothes. They will also send you up-to-date money-off vouchers and details of offers available at stores and online.

774 SPLIT THE COST

If you and your friends have a similar style and are around the same size, why not buy some clothes together and set a rota for sharing them? This works especially well when you are purchasing more expensive pieces that you know you won't wear all the time.

775 LOVE AT FIRST SIGHT

You should never buy something unless you totally love it. If you don't feel fantastic in a garment when you first try it on, you will be even less likely to want to wear it two months on.

776 NEVER SETTLE FOR 'IT'LL DO'

It's easy when you're looking for a particular style or item to settle for something that's nearly right instead of just perfect. But it's also a waste of money. If you can't find what you need by the end of the trip, don't be tempted to pick up just any old thing – go home, reassess the situation and begin a fresh hunt the next day.

777 SECOND TIME AROUND

A new invite doesn't necessarily mean you have to buy another outfit. Look at what you have already in your wardrobe and see if you can wear different pieces together to create a new look. If you are really struggling, buy only one new piece to add to the outfit, such as a top to wear with a favourite skirt or a pretty cardigan.

778 CHARITY-STORE FASHION

Charity shops can be great places to find a bargain provided you have the time to enjoy a good rummage through stock. Due to the rise in throwaway fashion, charity shops are now full of high-street clothes that have only been worn a few times. There's also the chance that you might find real hidden treasures without the worry that everybody else will be wearing the same clothes.

779 HIRE AN OUTFIT

If you've been invited to a black-tie event, hiring an outfit can be a cheaper alternative to buying one if you know you may never – or at least hardly ever – wear it again. What's more, you get the chance to wear an amazing designer frock for a night at a fraction of the price!

780 FIX YOUR PRICE

If you're on the lookout for a new outfit but are also restricted to a budget, take with you only the amount of money you want to spend so there's no possibility of you blowing your budget.

781 NO ONE NEEDS TO KNOW ...

A simple tip for saving money is to wear the same outfit to events with different people. Guests at a family wedding aren't to know that you wore exactly the same dress to a work event the week before.

782 LEGGING IT

Buying a new pair of funky tights is an instant way of creating a fashionable look that won't break the bank. The shops are full of legwear in every colour of the rainbow and as many patterns as you can think of. Be brave and show off your legs in style.

783 LET'S DO LUNCH

If your Saturdays consist of shopping and lunch out with a friend, have lunch together at home first so that you can talk away in peace and decide on what you want to buy that day. You can take it in turns to host and you'll easily save yourself money – which you can then invest in clothes instead.

784 BUY IN BULK

When shopping in boutiques and independent clothes stores you may find that if you ask nicely, the staff will give you a discount for buying more than one item. There's no harm in asking and they can only say no.

785 BORROW FROM A FRIEND

If you have a wedding or big night out coming up and don't want to buy a new dress, see if a friend has anything you can borrow instead. No one needs to know that it's not yours and you'll still feel as though you are wearing something new.

786 DAMAGED GOODS

If you discover that the piece of clothing you want to buy is damaged, before discarding it, assess whether it can easily be repaired without anyone knowing. If so, you should still buy it but make sure you tell the shop assistants and get yourself a discount.

787 RECYCLE YOUR WARDROBE

There's no need to buy new boots and coats every winter. If you go for classic shapes and good-quality material they won't date and will look their best for years to come. Keep leather boots looking smart with waterproof treatment and re-heel as soon as necessary. Keep coats in plastic covers to protect them from moths.

788 WORK IT

You will save money by buying tops, trousers and skirts that you can mix and match with the clothes you already have. Make sure the new item can be worn with at least two other pieces to save having to go out to buy more clothes.

789 FIND YOURSELF A STUDENT

Students are often given a discount in many of the leading high-street stores. But rather than trying to pass yourself off, give your money to a student friend and ask them to buy what you want using their discount – or drag student nieces, nephews or friends along when you want to go shopping!

790 LOOK CLOSE TO HOME

Fashion is always inspired by different eras and vintage has become a huge trend. But why spend money on retro pieces when you can get them for free? Ask female relatives for cast-offs from previous eras to enjoy the real thing.

791 SUPERMARKET SWEEP

Supermarkets don't just sell food – you can now buy great ranges of catwalk-inspired and up-to-the-minute clothes at unbelievable prices.

792 BIRTHDAY TREATS

Asking for vouchers from your favourite stores for birthday and Christmas presents is not only a way of avoiding unwanted gifts but it also means you can save them for when you are in need of a new pair of jeans or a coat.

DIY fashion

793 CUSTOMIZE YOUR CLOTHES

For an easy way to personalize a T-shirt without any sewing, look out for iron-on transfers at your local haberdashery store. Often they stock a whole variety of different transfers to suit the latest trends.

794 GIVE CLOTHES A SECOND CHANCE

Before you throw away an article of clothing, think about whether you can use the buttons or any of the trimmings on another top to give it a new lease of life.

795 MEASURE UP

Accurately measure yourself or ask a friend to help so that you know your exact measurements before you start sewing – it is also useful to take these measurements with you shopping to help with sizing. If you have a large enough piece of paper, have a friend to draw around you for an exact outline of your body to match the clothes up to.

796 MAKE YOUR OWN CLOTHES

Whether you want to save pennies or care about saving the environment, making your own clothes is the height of fashion. If you're a beginner, choose a dress pattern that consists of lots of straight stitching and doesn't have anything complicated like zips or pintucking. Wrap dresses and skirts are good options.

797 CUT IT OUT

When you're cutting out a pattern, always leave enough material for a little extra leeway. It's easier to get rid of excess material than to add it.

798 MACHINE MAGIC

Unless you're a whiz with a sewing machine, look for dressmaking evening classes at your local adult college to teach you the basic skills and to boost your confidence. Otherwise, ask someone who knows what they're doing to help you – it's lots of fun but mistakes can be expensive.

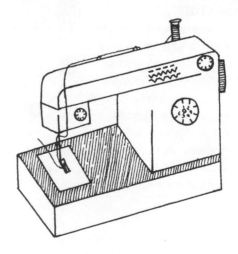

799 A STITCH IN TIME

Sew the garment together with loose hand stitches first and then once you've tried it on, you can easily make adjustments before sewing it with finished stitches.

800 DARING DENIM

Change an old pair of jeans into a denim skirt by cutting off the legs, then cutting up the inside legs and sewing them together. Or for an even easier option, simply cut off the legs where you desire for a pair of denim shorts.

801 CLEVER STUFF

If you have a favourite photo or an image on the Internet that you want to add to a top, print it off onto transfer paper (sold in haberdasheries and many stationery stores), which you can then iron directly onto your required top. Remember that you may have to rotate the item on the computer to ensure it comes out the right way on your garment.

802 HOMEMADE MASTERPIECES

You can customize jewellery, too. Add two pendants onto one necklace, or look in a bead shop for interesting and brightly coloured beads that you can thread with dental floss to make bracelets or necklaces (floss is much stronger than thread).

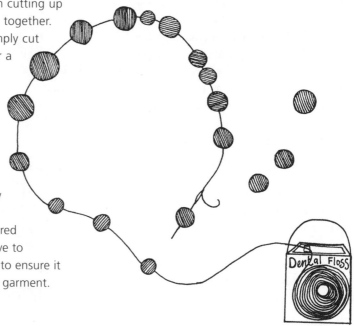

803 CREATE BY COMPUTER

If you don't feel confident enough to customize clothes yourself, there are plenty of different companies on the Internet who will do this for you. Most will create personalized jeans and tops – and some will even do shoes.

804 FASHION TO DYE FOR

Looking for a certain shade of clothing but can't find it anywhere? Try dyeing a plain white top or dress yourself to achieve the perfect colour.

805 TRAINER TASTE

Many of the big names in trainers (sneakers) offer a personalized service. You can choose your desired style, colour and even add a special message to the tongue or heel.

806 LACE ACE

Adding lace to sleeveless tops or dresses gives a touch of romance and femininity while also helping to hide unforgiving upper arms.

807 TIE A YELLOW RIBBON

Replace ugly bra straps with pieces of pretty coloured ribbon tied on the shoulder. Simply cut off or unpick the existing straps and sew on your desired piece of ribbon instead.

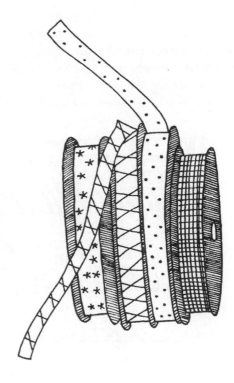

808 BIN BARGAINS

Most haberdasheries have remnant bins where they sell off cheaply pieces of material in odd shapes or the ends of lines. It's a great place to pick up fabrics you can use to customize clothes with, without having to spend money on more material than you need. If you're travelling, pick up pretty and vibrant pieces of fabric from souks or markets. You can instantly use them as belts or sarongs or create individual skirts and dresses that no one else has.

809 CUT IT OFF

If your jeans sit too high on your waist, cut off the waistband for a trendy, slim fit. A word of warning, however: this works best on jeans with button-flies rather than zippers.

810 BACK TO LIFE WITH A BOW

Give new life to a tired-looking little black dress by adding a wide, black silky ribbon to the waist and tying this in a big bow at the back.

811 IN THE NECK

Necklines are one of the easiest areas to customize. Cut across to make an off-the-shoulder top or if you are feeling extra brave, cut from one side of the neckline to under the sleeve on the other side for a single-shoulder look.

812 BELT MAKEOVER

Pick up plain belts from charity shops – you can paint on them or add studs or jewels and create a bespoke item.

813 GETTING SHIRTY

Raid your boyfriend's cupboard for old shirts that you can adapt. Cut off the sleeves, take in the sides and add a belt to create a casual dress that you can wear throughout the summer.

814 ADD SOME CHARM

Perk up a little clutch bag by adding a matching keyring or charm. You can buy gold, silver or leather ones from haberdashery departments in stores. The right one will make your bag look unique and chic.

vintage & second-hand clothes

817 VINTAGE SHOULD BE QUALITY

Just because an item is old does not mean it is vintage. Vintage clothing should possess a certain aesthetic quality that makes it stand out. Don't pay vintage prices for a 1980s T-shirt that many people will still have lurking at the back of their cupboards!

815 FLOWER POWER

A big flower corsage on a safety pin instantly transforms a plain black dress into a talking point. Coordinate the colour of the flower with the dress for a stylish look.

816 KEEP IT UP

When a strapless dress won't stay up, turn it into a flattering halter-neck. Sew strips of fabric onto the front to button up behind the neck.

818 MIX IT UP

Mix vintage with high-street items so you don't end up looking like you're off to a fancy-dress party.

819 REPAIR CARES

Make sure you thoroughly check the item of clothing you plan to buy. If it is very old it may have tears beyond repair or under-arm stains that cannot be removed.

820 FIND THE REAL THING

If buying designer vintage, do your research beforehand to make sure that you are buying the real thing. Check the authenticity by looking out for metal zips and buttons rather than plastic ones. Items of clothing produced after the 1970s will have a care label sewn inside.

821 ONLINE CAUTION

Be wary of buying vintage on the Internet. Ask the seller questions online to check the condition and the size of the garment. Sizes have changed a lot over the years so a size 10 item from the 1950s may actually be the equivalent of an 6 nowadays. Ask the seller to measure the item with a tape measure before you buy.

822 KNOW THE LINGO

Brush up on vintage clothing world language. If a piece is in 'mint condition' it means the item is rare, flawless and as near to its original state as possible while 'very good condition' means wearable but with some flaws.

823 WRAP WITH CARE

Check how your vintage clothing should be washed and stored. If in doubt, always dry-clean it, and wrap very delicate items in acid-free tissue to prevent damage.

824 VANITY FAIR

Keep an eye out for vintage fairs coming to your area. They are often run by professional vintage stallholders, which means you will have an array of choices all under one roof.

825 CLASSIC ACCESSORIES

A great way to add a touch of vintage to a new outfit is through a bag or jewellery. Look out for statement brooches or rings in the classic style of your favourite era.

826 SWEET CHARITY

Think about the location you shop in for second-hand clothes and try scouring the charity shops in smarter areas. The richer the place, the more expensive the clothes that are discarded – and the bigger the bargain for you!

827 HIGH QUALITY COUNTS

Look at the fabric before you buy and where possible purchase vintage clothes made of the highest quality. Natural fabrics hang better, last longer and look more expensive. This is particularly important if you are buying clothes made after the 1960s, when synthetic materials became increasingly popular.

828 TIMING IS EVERYTHING

Likewise, consider your timing, too. Charity shops are always full of clothes after Christmas and New Year and at the end of any season.

829 THE REAL THING

Study what's in fashion at the moment and then find the real deal. If the designers are using the 1950s as their inspiration, look for a full fifties skirt or a twinset.

830 GO FOR CLASSICS

When buying vintage or second-hand clothes go for classic shapes and colours that you can wear from year to year.

831 MAKE IT YOUR OWN

Try customizing second-hand clothes to bring them up to date with the latest trends. Add some different buttons or cut the sleeves off a man's shirt and finish off with a belt for an up-to-the minute look at half the price.

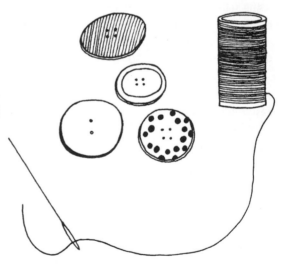

832 BID FOR IT

If you are looking for a real statement piece, consider buying at auction. Many celebrities and socialites sell off their pieces for charity and you can bag an original worn by an original.

833 GET IT ON

Always try on second-hand purchases, especially if they are old. Body shapes have changed over time, so while clothes from the 1950s may flatter curves, 1920s-style dresses are likely to suit a more boyish figure.

834 SPLASH OUT FOR LONGEVITY

If you can afford it, it's worth splashing out on designer vintage clothes as they do not lose their value over the years. They will be high-quality and become a talking point at parties.

835 GOING IN CIRCLES

Fashion always seems to work in cycles so look for staple second-hand items that can be reworked when the style becomes fashionable again.

836 TAKE YOUR TIME

Second-hand clothes buying is all about taking time to rummage through the rails to find a gem, so make sure you set aside plenty of time for the job. It's unlikely that you will be able to get your money back once you've made your purchase, so make sure you absolutely love the items you find.

837 SCRATCH AND SNIFF

Give vintage and second-hand clothes a subtle sniff before buying them. Odours such as from cigarettes cling to fabrics like leather and are almost impossible to get rid of.

838 IF ALL ELSE FAILS, FAKE IT

Love the clothes but can't afford the prices? Many fashion companies have recognized the growing market for vintage looks and have brought retro fashion back to the shops by using patterns from previously popular styles. Look out for old patterns in charity shops or at car boot (garage) sales, too.

stylists' secrets

839 BE A 'WAISTER'

Top stylists know that the best way to give any star instant glamorous curves is to accentuate the waist. Look for wide waist belts to wear over skirts and coats to create the illusion of a womanly hourglass figure.

840 NO SWEAT

The most expensive frocks can be spoilt by embarrassing sweat patches so the stars plan ahead to prevent perspiration marks at red-carpet events. Their favourite solution is a jab of Botox, which paralyses overactive glands to stop sweating. Less drastic are the powerful 24-hour deodorants (available from pharmacies).

841 SPRAY AROUND

To prevent a boob tube moving around too much or to stop ankle straps falling down on shoes, simply spritz hairspray on the inside before you go out.

842 ANTI-STATIC

Hairspray also works wonders by preventing static clothes from clinging to each other. Try spraying a little over your tights to stop a silky skirt or dress from sticking to them.

843 REMOVE STATIC WITH A HANGER

For skirts or dresses that have static cling, put the garment on, then reach up inside it with a metal hanger and brush the inside of the garment from top to bottom. For trousers, mould the hanger into a longer shape and reach up inside each trouser leg, brushing downwards.

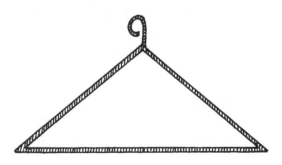

844 BE DISCREET

Don't show off more than you intend to when wearing revealing necklines. Invest in some double-sided fashion tape (often called 'toupee' tape) from department stores. Just stick some to the inner neckline of the dress and this will secure it firmly to your skin so your modesty remains intact all night!

845 SCRAP YOUR STYLE

Part of a stylist's job is to visit all the fashion shows, which is hardly possible for us mere mortals! Try keeping a scrapbook of models and famous people wearing great combinations of clothes to use as inspiration for what to buy.

846 NEVER BE OFF-DUTY

Stars look fabulous even when they're snapped just out grabbing a coffee. They know dressing down doesn't mean looking like a slob. Maxi dresses and wedges or well-fitting jeans with a distressed-look T-shirt are the LA wardrobe staples for a thrown-together but fabulous look.

847 STRAP IN

Paint a thin line of eyelash adhesive onto your shoulders when wearing spaghetti straps to prevent them from falling down all night.

848 SHINE ON

For a touch of instant evening glamour, stars often apply highlighter to their shoulders and décolletage as it catches the light and gives a healthy glow and slimming sheen.

849 BEAT THE BLOAT

If you have a big upcoming event but are suffering from a bloated tummy, keep off the carbs and salt for 24 hours beforehand. Drink herbal teas such as dandelion and fennel (natural diuretics that make you pee more!) and eat leafy green vegetables.

850 GET A SEAL OF APPROVAL

Stars have a whole crew of people to tell them if they look good. Similarly, enlist a few trusted friends to ask their opinions on a dry run before a big event.

851 KNOW YOUR HEEL HEIGHTS

Any stylist worth her salt knows that the combination of shoes with trousers can make or break a red-carpet outfit. For wide-legged trousers you need a heel or a wedge to elongate the leg, but skinny trousers best suit a classic ballet pump or flat boots over the top.

852 ACQUIRE PERFECT POSTURE

Ever wondered why stars and supermodels always have such an amazing presence? It's because of their posture. Hold your head high by imagining there is a vertical bar running between each ear and shoulder and between your chin and your chest bone. To make sure your pelvis is in line, pretend an elastic band is stretched between your belly button and tailbone and try to make it shorter.

853 BE WHITER THAN WHITE

White jeans can be a good look for summer but stylists know that they should only ever be worn with very specific underwear – nude thongs.

854 BEST FOOT FORWARD

Stars look great in photos because they stand with one leg forward and their foot pointed toward the camera. Their back foot takes their body weight so they're standing almost sideways on. This creates the illusion of a slimline figure.

855 DON'T GILD THE LILY

There's no easier way to ruin an outfit than by wearing too many accessories. One stylist secret is to look for a single statement piece and let that do the talking. If you just can't decide, put on all the accessories you want to wear, then look in the mirror and halve that amount.

856 MILLION-DOLLAR BABY

How is it that the stars manage to make high-street clothes look a million dollars? It's because they mix them with more expensive but also better-quality garments. Spend a large part of your budget on classic pieces in well-made fabrics and pick up on-trend high-street garments season to season.

857 THE FINAL TOUCHES

Stylists know that even the best outfit will be ruined if the wearer isn't beautifully groomed – that means a manicure, pedicure, waxing and a blow-dry before every special occasion.

858 STRIKE A POSE

Models know how to make the best of their faces before a camera because they have had so much practice. Spend some time studying your face in a mirror to see which is your best side and whether you look better pulling a big wide smile, and at which height your chin looks best. Better still, put this into practice by pulling some poses in front of a digital camera with a friend.

859 KEEP ABREAST OF THINGS

If you don't have a very large chest then you can fake it temporarily with 'chicken fillets' – silicon-filled pads you pop into your bra. Many stars are smaller than they look but rely on cleverly padded bras to create an enviable cleavage.

860 FIND YOUR STYLE GROOVE

Stylists make their clients look good because they know what styles suit them. Spend a day trying on different styles and when you find the perfect one for you, stick to it and only vary the colour, material and pattern – it's what all the leading Hollywood ladies do. Look at Liz Hurley – she's stuck to the same split-to-thigh, cleavage-revealing frocks for years.

861 STRAP-FREE, BUT SEXY

No stylist would ever dream of putting a top star in a strapless dress without a sturdy and flattering strapless bra. Not all strapless bras are created equal, however: a good one should create a great cleavage and uplift, too – not just hold your chest in place.

862 PRACTICE MAKES PERFECT

If you don't wear them often, practise walking around in high heels. Keep your weight shifted to your heel so you don't feel as if you might topple over, and take long, confident strides.

863 BE CLEVER WITH COLOUR

Stars look great because they (or their stylists!) know how to mix colours. If you're wearing black and primary colours together, accessorize and add in another colour to tone in and make the outfit look less like a uniform.

864 THEME IT

Stylists often work to a theme when dressing the rich and famous (cool and elegant, country chic, etc) so do the same when you get dressed in the morning. Think carefully about what you'll be doing. Will you have to walk far? Do you need layers for being inside and out? What will your surroundings be? What about a scarf to dress up or down for the evening?

865 SPLIT THE COST

Being a stylist is all about borrowing clothes. Do the same – but from your friends. Pinch pieces you know will suit you, or if you have seen a designer item but can't afford it, see if a friend might split the cost so you can share it between you.

866 SCAN FOR UNIQUE PIECES

Stylists want their clients to look like individuals not clones, so they pick up beautiful and interesting pieces from different countries and cultures. Do the same with a leather bag from South America or an armful of bangles from India to stand out from the crowd.

867 DIAMOND DAZZLE

There is truth in the saying that diamonds are a girl's best friend – which is why stars drape themselves in them at award ceremonies. If you can afford to buy the real thing, they really are a worthwhile investment and will make you look effortlessly glamorous at any special event. Good replicas are also out there, however, for a fraction of the price.

868 TAPE IT UP

Buttons and slits won't sit? You can't beat fashion tape! It adheres to your skin and lies flat when you press it onto the seam of an outfit, keeping unruly buttons and fabric in line.

869 BE TRUE TO YOURSELF

Stylists can suggest clothes but they know that if their clients don't feel comfortable in them, they won't look good. Fashion should be about wearing clothes you love and that make you feel a million dollars.

870 AVOID TACKY FASHION

Don't wear one designer from head-to-toe during the day unless you want to look like a wannabe. Wear a mixture of designer and high street and keep your flashier pieces for the evening.

871 GOOD SHOE SENSE

Any stylist knows that mixing black shoes with bright colours will only make the outfit look cheap. Keep black shoes for darker colours and if in doubt, wear shoes in a neutral shade.

872 TWINKLE, TWINKLE ...

Do as the stars do and wear long chandelier-style diamanté earrings at night – not only do they look elegant, they also catch the lights and sparkle as you move.

873 AVOID 'OUTFITS'

Have you noticed how the stars always mix and match on the red carpet? Outfits in which the skirt and top or dress and jacket are made to match look too contrived. Wearing stylish separates that coordinate is far cooler.

874 CUT A DEAL

Act like a true stylist and build up your contacts by getting to know the sales people at your favourite stores. If you have an existing relationship with them, they will be more likely to tell you when new deliveries arrive and sales events are coming up. Plus, you might find they offer you extra reductions or money off when you purchase multiple items.

875 THE PERFECT FIT

You won't find stars wearing baggy, ill-fitting clothes so you shouldn't either. Find a great tailor and have them accurately fit jackets, trousers and dresses. And learn to be handy with a safety pin – all stylists swear by them.

876 BE A BLACK-AND-WHITE BABE

Forget the old adage that says black and brown don't match – any stylist will tell you they do and they look sophisticated. Pair rich brown wool trousers with a black turtleneck, or for evening try a brown cocktail dress instead of black and dress it up with black beaded necklaces and bracelets.

877 LONG-LEGGED ILLUSION

A top-secret tip from stylists for making your legs look thinner is that they put their clients in nude-coloured shoes, which makes their legs appear endlessly long. Nudes and beiges also works well with clothes in most colours.

878 DON'T BE A HANGER-ON

You don't judge a book by its cover so don't judge clothing by how it looks on the hanger. If an item catches your eye but you're unsure about the shape, try it on before you reject it. You may discover a whole new look and open up your fashion horizons. Likewise, what might look great hanging up doesn't always look so good on.

879 DON'T BREAK THE LINE

When getting dressed, think about creating one continuous, unbroken line with your silhouette. Separates should be seamless, without interruptions from too-tight waistbands, creases pulling across thighs on trousers or skirts, lumps from ill-fitting bras or peeking bra straps and thongs.

880 BEAUTY BEFORE AGE

Stylists recommend dressing for your style and shape first and your age second. Just because you're the other side of 40, this doesn't mean that if you have great legs or upper arms you should hide them behind yards of material.

881 FLATTEN YOUR TUM

For decades, magic or 'gripper' knickers have been a well-kept celebrity secret. All women hate their tummies sometimes, especially if an outfit is unforgiving, and these big control pants are a great solution. Just be sure to buy a pair that fits perfectly – too tight and they'll cut off your circulation, too loose and they won't do their job.

882 FLAB SOS

If a celebrity has unexpectedly put on a few pounds before a red-carpet event, the stylist will resort to dressing them in an old faithful – a dark-coloured long dress with good classic lines that skim rather than hold onto curves. Invest in a gorgeous, flattering take-me-anywhere dress to do the same.

883 DRESS DOWN A FROCK

Get more mileage out of your eveningwear by dressing it down for the day. For example, add a cardigan and flat ballet pumps to a softly gathered 'goddess' frock for a romantic day look.

884 BECOME A QUEEN OF REINVENTION

The most fashionable stars continuously reinvent themselves. Stylists guide their clients away from fashion ruts by introducing them to new designers they wouldn't normally try. Do the same, by going into shops you normally avoid. Try on clothes you've never considered before, be bold and experiment … Who knows what great look you might end up with?

avoiding fashion faux pas

885 AVOID TOO-SHORT SKIRTS

It might look sexy, but if you don't feel comfortable you will be continuously trying to tug the hemline down. As a test, make sure you can sit down without worrying about what parts of your body you're exposing.

886 TOO TIGHT

Nothing makes you look bigger than squeezing into clothes clearly too small for you. It can also make you look older and 'dated'. Always wear your real clothes size.

887 TOO LOOSE

Another common mistake is to wear baggy clothes to try and hide excess weight, but be warned: this simply adds even more pounds! Instead, accentuate your positive points and show off your curves. Fitted tops and trousers are far more flattering than over-sized tent-like dresses.

888 MID-CALF BOOTS

Unless you are very tall, mid-calf boots tend to 'cut' legs in half, making them look short and a little stumpy.

889 ALL MIXED-UP

Don't make the mistake of trying to satisfy everything that is currently in fashion with one outfit. You will only look as if you're trying too hard. Stick to one style at a time.

890 DITCH THE CROP TOP

This style should only be worn by those aged under 18 with washboard abs. Even skinny girls often find they have a roll when they sit down in a crop top.

891 CREASED-UP MESS

What's the point in spending hours choosing the perfect outfit only to wear it crumpled? No clothes look good wrinkled, no matter how expensive they are, so always keep a good steam iron handy. If you really hate ironing, buy clothes that are made from fabrics which don't crease as much.

892 HIGH-HEEL BOOTS

Stick to flat boots if you have to walk any distance and don't wear ones with killer heels to daytime events or you'll spend the whole day tottering around with aching feet.

893 VPLS

A great outfit can be ruined by visible underwear, so invest in some well-fitting, streamlined smalls. If pants still show, your trousers or skirt are probably too tight!

894 SUNNY SLOB

Going on holiday is no excuse to slob out! Keep your standards up and don't wear tired and worn T-shirts or old clothes just because no one you know will see you. You'll feel dowdy and won't enjoy your break as much.

895 THE WRONG ACCESSORIES

Always top off your look with accessories that match your style. Choose the correct length necklace to suit the neckline of your top or dress. And never wear necklaces over the top of sweaters!

896 WATCH OUT WITH WHITE TROUSERS

White trousers can look terrible unless you are slim, so only wear them during the height of summer and if they are loose-fitting and made from a good-quality fabric that is not see-through.

disaster SOS

897 LADDERED TIGHTS

Always carry clear nail polish in your handbag – paint it on to stop surprise runs in their tracks. To prevent future ladders, make sure your tights are big enough – too small and they are more likely to rip.

898 EMERGENCY HEEL REPAIR

If a high heel snaps in two, coat one piece with a superglue (such as 'shoe goo') at the site of the break and try to reattach the other section. Stay off your feet as much as possible until you can change into another pair of shoes.

899 MEND A HEEL PROFESSIONALLY

Stop at a heel bar and see if there is anything that can be done to rescue your shoe – mending is best left to a pro. Failing that, visit your nearest shoe store and buy a pair. Ideally, keep fabric ballet pumps in your handbag for such emergencies.

900 RED WINE ON WHITE COTTON

Ask the barman or party host for soda water – it's the best thing for gently sponging off a red wine stain. Better still, play it safe and stick to black at parties where you know the alcohol is free-flowing!

901 MAKE PILES DISAPPEAR

If you're in a hurry, run a cool iron over the worst of the bobbled areas – this will flatten them – or draw a strip of Velcro along the piled fabric to remove the bobbles. Then, when you have time, invest in a pile shaver or pile razor (available from haberdashery departments) and shave your sweaters!

902 SHINE YOUR SHOES

Off to an important interview but you've scuffed your shoes? Smear a small amount of petroleum jelly over the toes and heels. It'll work until you can give them a proper polish.

903 SNAPPED HANDBAG STRAP

Rescue the strap by knotting it back onto your bag until it can be re-stitched. If it's not salvageable, try cutting off the other strap and carrying it as a hand-held purse until it can be replaced. To reduce the likelihood of this happening again, once a week clear out your bag to make sure you're not carrying around lots of unnecessary, heavy junk.

904 CHEWING-GUM STAIN

Remove as much of the gum as possible with a knife and then hold an ice cube to the stain until it hardens. You should then be able to scrape off the excess. Finally sponge the area with hot water.

905 GIVE ANIMAL HAIR THE BRUSH-OFF

If you don't have a clothes brush handy, sticky tape will work just as well. Wrap a strip over your hand and use it to pick up all the stray animal hairs.

906 RESCUE STUBBORN ZIPS

If a zipper simply won't budge, try running a lead pencil along the teeth. If that doesn't work, rub a bar of soap or a wax candle onto the problem area. With a little manipulation, it should come unstuck.

907 DEAL WITH SNAGS

Never cut a snag off as this will cause the garment to unravel. Instead, take a large darning needle, thread the tail and pull the snag inside. When you get the chance, sew it inside properly.

908 RUB AWAY RAIN MARKS

Use a nail file or rough pencil eraser to gently rub away rain marks from suede, being careful not to damage the delicate surface. This should ease out the stains. Also invest in a suede protector spray and apply a layer over your shoes or jacket every couple of weeks.

909 DON'T BE A CLING-ON

Most often, static occurs when you're wearing a skirt. For a quick fix, rub hand cream onto your thighs (over hosiery, if necessary). You can buy anti-static spray from the haberdashery section in department stores to apply to the inside of your skirt as well.

910 FASHION FIRST AID

Make your handbag a mini quick-fix kit to cope with any emergency. Stock it with a small bottle of clear nail polish, a tiny roll of sticky tape, a nail file, a mini pair of scissors and a spare pair of tights to cover most eventualities.

911 SLIPPING BRA STRAPS

Use 'toupee' tape (double-sided fashion tape) to stick your bra strap to your shoulder, or if you have time, nip into a lingerie store and buy a couple of bra clasps. These are attached at the back and then you pull the two back straps together – but you may still need a friend to help you.

912 BROOCH THE SUBJECT

Pop a large jewelled brooch into your handbag – you'll be amazed at what you can use it for. It can conceal a missing button, hide a stain, hold up trousers with a broken zipper, hide tears in clothes and transform a day bag into an evening one.

913 VARNISH IT

Always carry a bottle of the nail polish colour in the shade you are wearing, especially if it's a dark one. You can repair small chips on toes and fingers, and while this is not as good as a re-varnish, it looks a million times better than having the chip showing.

care & cleaning of clothes

914 BUTTON UP TIGHT

A loose button can quickly turn into a missing one, so dot the top with a little clear nail polish to prevent threads loosening further and the button completely falling off. Sew it back on as soon as you get the chance.

915 IT'S A STICK-UP

Sticky tape can pin up a dropped hem when you're out and about – but only temporarily. Use small bits at intervals rather than one long piece around the skirt or trouser bottom.

916 BE A BABE

Baby wipes are great for removing or reducing make-up stains on clothing. They also come in handy for getting rid of lint from clothing and dirt from shoes. Do not try to remove any stains from silk, though – this needs to be taken to a dry-cleaner.

917 BOOB MISHAPS

If the weather's chilly or you're going topless, try nude nipple covers to hide the view; alternatively try plasters (band-aids).

918 STIFF AND STARCHY

It might sound like a tip from the 1950s but using starch spray on cottons and linens helps keep their shape and prevents them from creasing as much. And it'll give your collars and cuffs a nice crisp finish, too.

919 INSIDE OUT

Turn jeans and denim jackets inside out to help prevent fading when you're washing. This goes for dark cords and bright-coloured cotton trousers, too.

920 EMPTY YOUR POCKETS

The first rule of machine washing is to make sure you empty all the pockets on clothes – there's nothing worse than unloading a dark wash only to discover everything is covered in white bits from the tissue you left in your jeans pocket!

921 HANG AROUND

Clothes that can't be tumble-dried should be placed on hangers to dry naturally. Do this immediately after they come out of the machine to reduce ironing time.

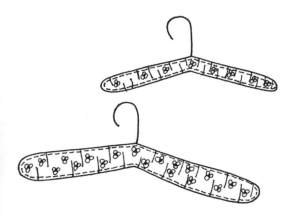

923 GOOD HOUSEKEEPING

To avoid last-minute panics in the morning, set aside one hour a week to iron, organize dry-cleaning and sew on buttons or tidy up hems, and so on.

922 COLD RINSE

A common mistake when hand-washing clothes is to use hot or warm water, but even this may damage delicate fabrics. Always use cold water and don't ever leave items to soak or they may shrink.

924 FLAT AND DRY

Wool loses its shape if hung out to dry. The best thing to do is to roll items in a towel to absorb excess water and then lay them out flat to dry, keeping them away from sources of direct heat such as radiators.

925 CLEAN DELIVERY

Check out your local dry-cleaning delivery service. Most residential areas and many larger offices have them. They make life easier by picking up and dropping off items at a time convenient to you.

926 BIT OF FLUFF

Remember, any clothes that shed – such as towels and fleeces – should be washed separately to avoid covering everything else with fluff.

927 SMOOTH AND SILKY

Some silk can be hand-washed in lukewarm water with a gentle detergent, while other silks must be delicate dry-cleaned. Add a few drops of gentle fabric conditioner to the final rinse to prevent static. Silk dries very quickly and shouldn't be tumble-dried or placed on a radiator. Steam-iron carefully by placing a cloth over the silk to protect it, thus avoiding direct contact with the iron.

928 KEEP IT CLEAN

Never iron clothes that are stained as the heat may seal in the stain and make it harder to remove. Anything delicate should be ironed on the reverse, or use a cloth laid over the fabric to protect it.

929 OLD-FASHIONED WASH DAY

Make one evening a week 'wash night'. It may sound boring but think how pleased you'll be not to have the situation where the top you really want to wear is dirty. Make it more fun by playing your favourite CD or chatting to a friend on your hands-free as you go.

930 SHRINKING VIOLETS

All wool shrinks at high temperatures so always check the label before you put it in the machine. Cashmere and similar delicate knits should be hand-washed, regardless of what the label says.

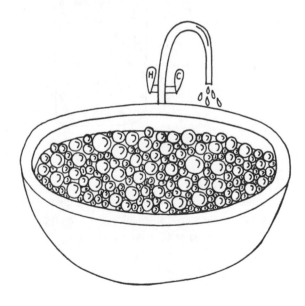

making high fashion wearable

932 HIT A KEY NOTE

Instead of trying to copy a catwalk trend from top to bottom, pick out one key piece that will take you through the whole season and beyond. A great pair of on-trend shoes is a safer buy than a statement dress that you can only wear once and will be copied in all the high streets stores before you know it.

933 DON'T BE A DEDICATED FOLLOWER

Remember that fashion trends work in opposites – low-rise trousers give way to high waists; skinny jeans hail the advent of the palazzo's return. So to be truly ahead of your time, start wearing a style's opposite partner just as the look hits the mainstream. People will think you are very stylish and a trendsetter rather than follower.

931 SUBTLE SCENT

Scented waters such as lavender are a great way to infuse subtle smell into your clothing. Add scented water to an iron on steam setting and gently waft it over clothing. This is a great way to freshen clothes that have been in storage for a few months.

934 V IS FOR VERSATILITY

Study the main silhouettes of the season and spend a bit more money on a piece of clothing in one of those shapes that you can take from day to night – just add a pair of heels and some smart accessories.

935 PLAY IT SAFE

If you want to make just one high-fashion investment, go for a great coat or jacket – it will be the first thing people see, so pick one to suit your shape and colouring that you can rely on year after year.

936 TURN HEADS WITH CONFIDENCE

The key to wearing a high-fashion statement piece is to wear it with the confidence it deserves. Stand tall with your shoulders back to show off what you are wearing. You'll turn heads, so enjoy it!

937 MIX 'N' MAX

Combine designer pieces with high-street garments to dress up or play down an outfit – it will save money and make items more versatile.

938 LOOK FOR SPIN-OFFS

An increasing number of designers are extending their ranges to provide a cheaper version of their high-end fashion. Alternatively, look for collaborations between high-fashion designers and high-street stores to get a designer piece for a fraction of the cost.

939 CATWALK TO HIGH STREET

If you like a designer piece but don't want to pay the high prices, the good news is that you don't have to go without – or even wait. The average time from catwalk to high street is now as little as two to three weeks, so you can pick up a designer-inspired number that looks almost as good for a fraction of the price.

940 BUILD UP SLOWLY

Pay attention to what the latest trend for the upcoming season will be – such as frills or tartan prints – and buy one or two key pieces that fit into your own style. You can always add to this as the season continues if you find you're wearing the look a lot.

941 LOOK FOR DESIGNER DAY DRESSES

A one-piece day dress looks effortlessly chic and the bonus of buying designer is that the cut and fabric will be amazing so you'll look and feel great. Choose shirt-dresses in cotton or wrap dresses in heavy jersey – both are easily dressed up or down and won't date.

942 PICK WISELY

Just because designers are sending a certain look down the catwalk, this doesn't mean it will suit everyone. If you are unsure about a style, you could end up looking uncomfortable and not get your money's worth out of the item – so be sure it flatters your shape and isn't just on-trend.

943 THINK CLASSIC CHIC

If you're splashing out on a designer piece, choose something that will last longer than one season. A classic little black dress can be worn again and again while that fluorescent print may be pushed to the back of the wardrobe after a couple of wears.

944 START SMALL

Work your accessories to the max. A designer-inspired scarf or necklace can provide an effortless way of showing you've got the real thing without paying out too much cash.

945 BE AGE AWARE

Ageing is a fact of life and there are just some trends – such as micro minis, tummy-flaunting tanks and cleavage-revealing tops – that are only right at a certain age. You don't have to show skin to be contemporary – look out for trends that suit any age.

946 FOCUS ON ONE

Choose one trend and make it your focus. If you're wearing a peasant skirt, boots, a wide belt, a chunky wooden necklace and chandelier earrings simultaneously, you might want to reconsider and pare down a little – the different pieces will simply cancel each other out, blotting out their individuality.

947 WEAR IT RIGHT

Some trends require preparation work. For example, if you're going to tuck your jeans into your boots, you have to do a little more than slap them on over jeans otherwise your jeans will bunch up like lopsided accordions. For a sleek and fabulous look, wear straight-leg jeans so there's less excess material to squeeze into the boot, and before putting your boots on, tuck your trouser legs securely into your socks.

948 GET AN IDOL

Forget the catwalk or magazines, if there's a look you love, study the style and clothes of a real person you admire – either a celebrity or someone you know who's über-stylish – and then adapt it to suit you.

949 OWN YOUR TREND

To avoid looking like a fashion victim, be in charge of the trend you choose. After all, if you're not the owner of your look, who is? Wear it as if it's a part of your very essence, an extension of your personality.

950 STAY SYMMETRICAL

When considering which trends work for you, study the proportions of both the garments and your body. Gaucho pants and voluminous skirts might be trendy, but they need to be balanced out by the rest of your outfit or you could look like you're wearing a sack. Pair full shapes from the waist down with chunkier shoes or boots and form-fitting tops to give a sense of symmetry to the silhouette.

951 DON'T BE SCARED OF THE CATWALK

Seen it on the runway and you're intrigued yet a bit intimidated? Don't be put off by outrageous trends at shows. These looks will be altered and softened for the customer piece. For instance, dresses are made shorter and tighter, bodices more revealing and scarves fuller and longer than anyone could imagine pulling off on an ordinary day. So don't be deterred if a trend appears outrageous at first sight – by the time it hits the stores, it will have been modified for real life.

213

ageless style

952 KEEP YOUR WARDROBE UP-TO-THE-MINUTE

Wearing former trends only points out exactly how old you are, so keep up with the latest fashions by buying at least one key piece each season that suits your age and body shape.

953 FLATTER WITH COLOUR

Certain shades can be more ageing than others. To find out your most flattering colours try holding a light blue, a royal blue, an orange and a peach colour next to your skin and see which makes you look youngest. If it's royal blue you should stick to black, white and primary colours, while light blue means your colours are grey, white and pastels. If orange made you look the youngest, autumn colours such as gold, coral, ivory and earth tones are the best suited, and finally, if the peach colour looked best, warm pastels and ivories are the least ageing colours for you.

954 FIGHT GRAVITY

As gravity takes its toll on the body, fake your way back to your 20-year-old shape with good support. Look for underwear that lifts, holds and tucks everything back into its original place.

955 DITCH THE GRANNY SHOES

The older we get, the more we prefer comfort over style, but when it comes to choosing shoes, avoid frumpy ones – court shoes in particular can really age you. Instead of trainers or boring, flat lace-up shoes, go for slightly smaller but delicate heels, chunky but smart boots and pretty ballet pumps.

956 SAY IT WITH COLOUR

While black is a fail-safe colour that can look very sophisticated as you get older, be wary of wearing it from head to toe. Team it with softer, darker colours such as deep purple or burgundy and avoid wearing too much black near your face as it can make you look sallow and draw attention to under-eye bags.

957 RAISE YOUR WAIST

After having kids your waistline often becomes less defined, so create the illusion of a waist through higher-waisted jeans and Empire-line tops that make your waistline look higher than it is.

958 BANISH THE BAGGY

Don't think that just because you're not 21 anymore, your clothes should become baggier. Garments that are well tailored and fitted will always be more flattering and make you look instantly fashionable.

959 COVER TELL-TALE SIGNS

The upper arms and the neck are prone to revealing your age, so if you hate these areas on you, cover them up with scarves, shawls and sleeves.

960 SEX APPEAL

Looking glamorous doesn't mean having lots of bare skin on display. Show off your sensuality through fabrics such as silk, cashmere and leather in rich and sumptuous colours.

961 UPDATE YOUR JEANS

Keep an eye on which styles of jeans are in each season and get rid of jeans in old-fashioned shapes. Darker denim bootcut jeans will be more flattering, and while you don't want to expose yourself in very low-rise jeans, be careful with very high-waisted ones, which can give you what's known as a flat 'mum bum'.

962 KEEP IT SIMPLE

Go for classic cuts and shapes rather than overly fussy and frilly clothes. Look for the classic staples such as trench coats and A-line dresses for sophisticated but on-trend chic.

963 DRESS YOUR SHAPE, NOT YOUR AGE

When it comes to buying clothes, choose fashions that suit and flatter you rather than what you think is appropriate for your age. Don't hit a big '0' birthday and suddenly start wearing pearls and a twinset with camel trousers! If you've got the figure, wearing classics with a fashionable twist always works.

964 AVOID THE MATRON BAG

With so many gorgeous bags in the shops there's no excuse for a matronly 'Mary Poppins' bag that will add years to your look. Classic shapes and well-made leather bags look far more chic on older women than they do on the young.

965 ACCEPT THAT SOME CLOTHES AREN'T FOR YOU

Dressing in styles and shapes meant for very young women and teens won't make you look younger – even if you have a great body. Take inspiration from styles such as wearing short dresses over slim-line trousers but make them work for your age.

966 MOVE WITH THE TIMES

When you find a style that you feel comfortable with it's easy to keep to it, but check your look hasn't become dated. As you get older, what may have looked good on you in your 30s might not be the same when you hit your 40s. Keep looking fresh and fashionable by updating your look to suit you.

967 AVOID SHORT SKIRTS

There's nothing worse than wearing too-short skirts and dresses once you're past 30. If you have good legs, you can still show them off but do so with hemlines that stop around the knee or just below.

968 KEEP TO CLASSIC PRINTS

Going for a traditional print in muted shades rather than bold brash patterns is best for any age. Prints such as dogtooth and check are more flattering and won't make you look as if you're trying too hard.

969 BEAUTY IN SIMPLICITY

Too much make-up, jewellery and rock-solid hair-dos are a sure-fire way to age you. Always go for a more natural look and make-up – it's simple but effective.

970 BEWARE SCOOP AND ROUND NECKS

These are the least flattering necklines as they repeat the line of a drooping cleavage and highlight any crêpey skin. Instead, stick to v-necks, which draw the eye upwards for a more youthful effect.

971 TRENDY SPECS

Wearing glasses doesn't have to make you look older. Work out what shape suits your face and then look at the latest trend is for that style. Study magazines to see what celebrities are wearing and if you can, treat yourself to a designer pair.

972 KEEP UP THE MAINTENANCE

Never think that as you get older you shouldn't have to bother quite so much. In fact, it's the opposite. Although it may take a bit longer to look groomed, it's a sure-fire way to look stylish and younger for longer.

973 ESCAPE THE CHAIN GANG

Avoid chokers or necklaces on very short chains – they will draw attention to a lined neck. Go for longer statement pieces or pendants that fall in a v shape.

974 AVOID DANGLY EARRINGS

Long earrings will draw attention to a less-than-firm jaw line, especially if you're wearing your hair up. Opt instead for classic studs or small hoops.

975 LOOK FOR DESIGNERS' PEERS

When it comes to fashion, keep an eye on what designers of a similar age to you are doing. They will be creating with their contemporaries in mind and designing clothes to flatter and keep similar-aged women looking young and stylish.

976 ACCENTUATE YOUR SHOULDERS

Look for jackets with slight shoulder pads or structured shoulders as this will hide drooping shoulders and also balance out any middle-aged spread.

ethical fashion

977 30 IS THE NEW 40

By washing your clothes at 30°C (86°F) instead of 40°C (104°F) you'll save 40% of the usual electricity consumed, making this a greener option – plus your clothes will last longer.

978 THINK ABOUT FABRIC

Where possible, avoid clothes made with nylon and polyester. Not only are they non-biodegradable, making them difficult to dispose of, but both are made from petrochemicals that pollute the environment and add to the problem of global warming.

979 GO GREEN

Look for products made from organic cotton. This is grown without the use of chemical pesticides and insecticides and so saves money for the farmer while also saving the planet. Organic wool produced using sustainable farming practices and without toxic sheep dips is also increasingly sold in shops.

980 FAIRTRADE FASHION

It's not just coffee and chocolate that can be Fairtrade. Look for the Fairtrade mark on cotton clothing. This ensures that the cotton is made to Fairtrade standards, which means the farmers were paid fairly and had safe working conditions.

981 TA-TA TO TUMBLE DRYERS

The sun and wind do just as good a job of drying your clothes as any tumble dryer. Drying them outdoors – or inside on a rail if it's raining – saves energy and also makes your clothes smell far better than using a machine. Plus it avoids shrinkage and wear and tear.

982 PARTY ON!

A clothes-swapping party is not only a fun way to spend a night with your friends but you might also go home with a whole new wardrobe for free. Instead of throwing clothes away and adding to the endless piles of junk already filling up waste tips and landfill sites, swap them with friends of a similar size who want to offload their own unwanted clothes.

983 DYE DISASTERS

Try to avoid patent leather and the colour turquoise – both are very pollutant in terms of the chemicals they create during production. Copper in real turquoise dyes gets released into the environment through waste water.

984 CHARITY CHIC

Green, cheap and ethical, charity shops are often the ideal place to pick up a bargain. By buying (and taking) your clothes to charity stores, not only are you helping the environment but you are also giving to those in need.

985 HIGH-STREET ETHICS

Many of the big high-street chains are waking up to the demand for eco-friendly products and have launched their own organic ranges. Many now stock clothes made from organic cotton for only a fraction more than the price of their ordinary ranges.

986 GREEN PEACE OF MIND

Everybody likes a bargain but at what cost? Sometimes there are reasons why clothes are so cheap and often it's because they have been shipped over from China or India where costs of labour are a tiny amount of the price paid. Check out the policies of your favourite stores – sometimes it's worth paying a little more for peace of mind.

987 TRY A WET CLEANER

Conventional dry-cleaning often uses a toxic chemical that has been linked to cancer. In the US, some states including California have already started to phase out this chemical and replace it with healthier options. The best alternative is 'wet-cleaning', which costs the same but uses biodegradable soap instead of harsh chemicals. Ask your local dry-cleaner if they offer this service.

988 GET KNITTED

Knitting has become a trend on the film sets of many Hollywood productions with celebrities often snapped holding a pair of needles and a ball of wool. To be eco-friendly, unravel the wool from old sweaters or charity store finds and reuse it.

989 LEADER OF THE PACK

Hand-reared Alpaca hair is a greener alternative to conventional sheep's wool as it's spun locally and so keeps transport to a minimum. Look for sweaters made from this yarn on the Internet.

990 FRIENDLY FIBRES

The average cotton T-shirt requires 1168 litres (257 gal) of water to make, while the cotton industry itself uses 22.5% of all insecticides consumed globally. An eco-friendly alternative is to look for clothes made of hemp. Its naturally long fibres make it suitable for spinning with minimal processing and because it grows so densely, it's harder for weeds to grow and so there's no need for herbicides. Hemp clothing can be found on the Internet, as well as garments made from other eco-friendly materials such as soy silk and bamboo.

991 MAKE DO AND MEND

Put your grandmother's words into practice and do some simple alterations and repairs. The rise in cheap clothing has led to some people simply throwing away clothes that could easily be made as good as new with a little cutting and sewing. It's estimated that 500,000 tonnes of unwanted clothes end up on landfill sites every year. If you're not handy with the needle, find a tailor you trust and you'll be helping out local business at the same time.

992 DITCH THE FABRIC CONDITIONER

Clothes washed with conditioner are basically being pumped full of artificial fragrances and other potentially allergy-causing chemicals that also pollute the environment. For a natural fragrance, spritz with water containing a few drop of rose or lavender essential oil.

993 SHOP LOCAL

Help cut down on carbon emissions by buying clothes that are made locally. Many towns hold craft fairs throughout the year where talented designers and clothes makers sell their products and these are made without the use of cheap labour and often from materials much closer to home.

994 GET A 'GREEN' WEDDING DRESS

Because most wedding gowns are only ever worn once, it's worth considering eco-friendly options. Look for a style made from natural fibres such as organic cotton or hemp or for something more luxurious, try silk charmeuse. Alternatively, buy a vintage dress from your favourite era.

985 BUY LESS AND STYLE MORE

Try putting different pieces of clothing together or wearing something in a way that you haven't before – for example, a dress over trousers or a scarf as a belt – rather than always rushing out to buy new items.

986 THINK BEFORE YOU WASH

Don't throw clothes into the wash just because you've worn them once. Only wash them when they really are dirty – many stains can be removed with a little warm water.

987 OLD-STYLE GLAMOUR

Vintage clothing has become increasingly fashionable in recent years, allowing you to invest in one-off classic pieces while helping the environment at the same time. Many towns now have vintage shops – or look out for markets in your area.

988 WARDROBE REVAMP

Redesign the clothes you already have to bring them up to date with current trends. Shorten the hemline of an old dress or add a new set of buttons to a dated shirt.

989 FAKE IT

Fact: faux is in. There's no need for small, furry creatures to suffer for your style. In the last ten years, pretend fur has come a long way and is now used to adorn anything from boots to coats and hats – it's as beautiful and luxurious as the real thing, too.

1000 EARTH-FRIENDLY ACCESSORIES

More and more designers are making handbags and belts from recycled or sustainable materials. Check out bags made of recycled tyres and the latest handbag shapes in environmentally friendly natural fibres such as cotton, hemp and canvas.

1001 LEAVE LEATHER BEHIND

Follow in the footsteps of the rich and famous and buy a pair of vegan shoes or a vegan handbag. Actress Natalie Portman is a fan of elegant and stylish vegan shoes, while designer Stella McCartney is famous for only ever sending shoes made entirely without animal ingredients down the catwalk. Check the Peta website (www. peta.org) for vegan companies.